KENTUCKY
Sweets

BOURBON BALLS, SPOONBREAD & MILE HIGH PIE

SARAH C. BAIRD

Illustrations by CHASE CHAUFFE

AMERICAN PALATE

Published by American Palate
A Division of The History Press
Charleston, SC 29403
www.historypress.net

First published 2014

Manufactured in the United States

ISBN 978.1.62619.377.2

Library of Congress CIP data applied for.

To my parents, who will forever be more fun and interesting than I could imagine.

Contents

Part 4. Celebration Sweets

Part 5. Confections and Candies

Acknowledgements

First and foremost, my illustrator and friend Chase Chauffe, who has the unique combination of sensational talent and complete humbleness. I am constantly amazed by his work and look forward to our many projects.

Trevor Alan Taylor, who was so receptive and open to my (kind of wacky and) playful ideas for shooting the food, with an attention to detail that is unmatched.

The hundreds and hundreds of Kentuckians across the state whom I bombarded with questions, suggestions, ideas and queries into their personal sugar preferences.

In close, of course, I owe a mound of debt to the lovely and talented Kirsten Schofield and her colleagues at The History Press, without whom this book would not be possible in the most real sense.

Thank you all, from the bottom of my heart.

Introduction

Kentucky—arguably the first true wilderness to be tamed by explorers after the eastern seaboard became crowded—is also a land of rich and robust culinary heritage. The sugar-laden back roads and main streets of the commonwealth are ripe with stories just waiting to be told about how sweet traditions have helped to shape families and communities, from the sorghum-rich hills of eastern Kentucky to candy makers in the heart of urban Louisville.

Located at the intersection of the Midwest and South, the culinary traditions of Kentucky are unlike any other state in the nation. Combining the homey, cozy favorites of middle America with the South's flair for decadence and an Appalachian focus on homegrown, local ingredients, Kentucky is uniquely stubborn in its adherence to tradition and doggedly determined to preserve the foodways that have made it both inviting and intimidating since Daniel Boone first trailblazed through its woods.

This work focuses on a sampler (not Whitman's but still tasty) of baked goods, candies and sweets (and a few cocktails of course) from across the state, with anecdotes, oral histories and pop culture tidbits thrown in for good measure. Each of these sweets is deeply woven into the fabric of local communities and the state as a whole, from the hotly contested courtroom cases surrounding Derby Pie® to just why and how the Maysville favorite translucent pie differs from other regional chess pie variations.

Take a seat, grab a fork and dig in.

Part 1

FRUITS and NUTS

HICKORY BRITTLE

*I*t's sweet, it's earthy, it's rich…and it needs a better PR agent. If more folks knew about the buttery, delicious nature of a hickory nut, let's just say that the pecan and cashew would be getting pretty jealous over the new kid in town. Hickory trees are found all over the state of Kentucky, and their delicious interior—while a bit difficult to remove—is well worth the effort.

TOOL SPOTLIGHT: CANDY THERMOMETER

One of the biggest objections people have to tackling candy making is a deep fear of using a candy (or deep fry) thermometer. It's time that we put those fears to rest. For better or worse, math (ounces, pounds and grams, oh my!) is an integral part of cooking and baking. Why would you not want to use all the tools at your disposal—kitchen scales, thermometers and more—to ensure that your dish is going to come out just right? This isn't high school calculus, I promise.

Candy thermometers can be found in practically all supermarkets, but they are somewhat fussy instruments that can easily be knocked off kilter. After purchasing your thermometer, or if you dig one out of the dark reaches of a drawer, take the time to ensure that it is functioning properly. Clip the thermometer to the side of a baking pan and fill it with water, bringing the water in the pan to a boil. The thermometer should read 212°F. If your thermometer's reading doesn't measure up, it's probably time to invest in a new one.

Always use the thermometer's clip to your advantage while making candy in order to ensure the greatest accuracy, and do keep an eye on the mixture at all times. Candy typically cooks very slowly when boiling until it reaches 220°F, whereupon it rapidly speeds up. A close watch will ensure that the candy doesn't burn, leaving you with a charcoal-colored mess.

If disaster strikes in the middle of cooking and your thermometer breaks, always have an understudy close at hand so as to not disrupt the flow of the recipe.

After using your thermometer, allow it to cool completely before washing it to ensure that it does not break. Additionally, never put your thermometer in the dishwasher, as they can easily be knocked out of whack by the tossing and turning motions.

Hickory Nut Aliases
pig nut, king nut

Brittle Aliases
slab sugar candy

TIPS AND TRICKS

Crushing Nuts: Chopping nuts is no one's idea of an enjoyable pastime, especially when nuts can move from perfectly chopped to a filmy nut powder in a matter of errant strokes. If you don't have a food processor or mini-chopper at your disposal, get ready to go analog. Place the nuts in a zip-lock bag or between two pieces of plastic wrap. Seal the bag or the edges of the wrap and cajole the nuts into a single layer. Place the bag between two tea towels and, using a rolling pin, crush the nuts through the towel, checking regularly, until the nuts are in the desired piece sizes.

Brittle Battle: There's nothing more daunting than the thought of pulling molten candy mere seconds after it has ceased to bubble and spew. It's important, though, to bite the bullet and stretch the candy while it's still hot and pliable in order to make a thinner, crispier brittle. (I promise, you want that signature first snap of the candy.) After pouring the brittle into the prepared pans, wait about sixty seconds before beginning to pull. The most important part? Wear rubber gloves, preferably the heavy-duty yellow kind typically reserved for bathroom cleaning. Your safety and comfort is a priority, so don't be a tough guy and end up with third-degree sugar burns. When pulling, don't just grab from the edges but from the middle, too, to

make the brittle as thin as possible. The nuts should be just barely bound together with tender, crunchy candy.

In the Raw: Raw hickory nuts provide a much better flavor for the brittle than those that have been roasted, salted or otherwise doctored. If you use roasted nuts, however, add them at the end of the cooking time. If added too soon, roasted nuts could burn and leave the candy with a bitter taste.

Hickory in Song

"Hickory Wind" by Emmylou Harris
"Hickory" by Frankie Valli
"Hickory" by Iron and Wine

SIDEKICK RECIPE
BROWN SUGAR OATMEAL HICKORY COOKIES

Yield: about 20–25 cookies
Active Time: 15 minutes * Total Time: 30 minutes
Special Tools: handheld electric mixer

1½ cups hickory nuts, chopped
2 sticks unsalted butter
1½ cups dark brown sugar
2 large eggs, room temperature
1 teaspoon vanilla extract

1½ cups all-purpose flour
1 teaspoon baking powder
1 teaspoon ground cinnamon
1 teaspoon ginger
3 cups old-fashioned rolled oats

Preheat oven to 350°F. Chop the hickory nuts coarsely. (See "Tips and Tricks" for helpful hints.) In a large bowl, using a handheld electric mixer, cream together the butter and sugar until light and fluffy. Slowly add the eggs one at a time until fully incorporated, then mix in vanilla. In a medium bowl, sift together the dry ingredients. Beat dry ingredients into the butter-sugar mixture until smooth, making sure not to overmix. Fold in the oats and hickory nuts until evenly distributed. Using a melon baller or tablespoon, place cookie dough in evenly sized (roughly 1½ inches) mounds on greased cookie sheets. Bake 12–15 minutes, rotating the pans halfway through baking. Let stand for 1 minute on pan after removing from oven, then transfer to baking rack to cool.

SIDEKICK RECIPE
HICKORY TART

Yield: 1 9-inch tart
Active Time: 30 minutes * Total Time: 1 hour, 40 minutes
Special Tools: 9-inch tart pan, electric handheld mixer

For the Crust:

½ cup unsalted butter, room
   temperature
¼ cup sugar
1 egg yolk
⅛ teaspoon salt
1¼ cups all-purpose flour

For the Filling:

3 large eggs, room temperature
½ cup brown sugar
1 cup sorghum
¼ cup unsalted butter, melted
1 teaspoon vanilla extract
⅛ teaspoon salt
1½ cups hickory nuts, coarsely
   chopped

For the Crust:

Using an electric handheld mixer, beat butter until fluffy and creamy. Slowly add sugar, egg yolk and salt and beat until blended. Add flour and beat until dough clumps together. Turn dough into a ball and roll it out on a lightly floured surface. Press dough into tart pan and prick with fork along sides and bottom for ventilation. Place in freezer for a minimum of 1 hour.

For the Filling:

Preheat oven to 350°F. Whisk eggs and brown sugar until well blended. Whisk in sorghum, melted butter, vanilla extract and salt. Fold in the hickory nuts. Pour filling into prepared, unbaked crust. Bake until filling is slightly puffed and set, about 40 minutes.

SIDEKICK COCKTAIL
HICKORY BOURBON HOT TODDY

Yield: 1 cocktail

2 tablespoons clover honey
1½ ounces hickory-infused bourbon (see following)
1 cup boiling water
orange wedge, garnish

Rim the bottom and sides of an Irish coffee glass with honey. Add bourbon. Fill with boiling water and stir. Garnish with orange wedge.

Making Hickory-Infused Bourbon: Soak two cups of shelled, chopped hickory nuts in water to remove remaining shell and bitter flavor. Season with cinnamon and roast in an oven at 300°F for about 40 minutes. Combine nuts and four cups of high-quality bourbon in an airtight container. Allow mixture to soak for one week before use, straining to remove any rogue nut pieces.

HICKORY BRITTLE

Yield: 2 pounds
Active Time: 1 hour
Total Time: 1 hour, 30 minutes
Special Tools: candy thermometer, rolling pin,
10x15-inch baking sheets

2 cups granulated sugar

1 cup light corn syrup

1 cup water

1 tablespoon butter

2 cups hickory nuts, chopped

2 teaspoons baking soda

2 teaspoons vanilla extract

Grease baking sheets with butter and set aside. In a heavy-bottom saucepan with a candy thermometer attached, combine sugar, corn syrup and water. Cook and stir over medium heat until sugar dissolves. Continue cooking until mixture boils, then add butter. Continue cooking, without stirring, until mixture reaches "soft ball" stage, about 235°F. Begin stirring and continue to cook until the mixture reaches "hard ball" stage, 266°F. Add nuts, stirring constantly until the thermometer reads 300°F, then remove pan from the heat.

Working quickly, add baking soda and vanilla to the mixture, stirring until combined. Pour onto prepared baking sheets and spread candy until a roughly even thickness. Taking all proper safety precautions (see the "Tips and Tricks" section in this chapter) and using gloved hands, stretch the brittle until just thin enough to hold together the nuts. Break candy into pieces when cool and store in an airtight container.

Sweet Sound Off:
John Brittain
Owner, Nolin River Nut Tree Nursery

John Brittain is one of the premier experts on hickory nuts in the country, having operated his nut tree nursery—which focuses heavily on native Kentucky fruit and nut trees—for decades. Here, Mr. Brittain talks about the unique taste of the hickory nut, its place in Kentucky culture and just why it might be the perfect nut for baking.

Are you from the Nolin River area?
I'm not originally from Kentucky. I grew up in Evansville, Illinois, up by Chicago. I've been here for over forty years, though, so I've mainly lived in this area all my life.

Explain how you started the company. Were you always interested in trees?
I've always been really interested in the outdoors and nature and biology. I had a degree in biology and soil science, and I was teaching the local community college courses in chemistry, agriculture and biology back in the late '70s and early '80s. I was getting ready to plant some trees on my farm in Hart County, about sixty miles south of Louisville, and a friend of mine from college told me, "You ought to go see this man, Wes; he lives near you and grafts nut trees in his little nursery." So, coming home from teaching one day, I stopped by his place and introduced myself. We hit it off real well; he was retired and had been running a fruit nursery on the side while he was in the civil service. He and his brother had been looking for nut trees and were having trouble finding grafted nut trees at the time. That's what actually got them into experimenting with grafting nut trees, and he basically became my mentor. I'd stop by, and he'd show me what he was doing—I had the scientific background to know what was going on from a biological perspective—and he had the hands-on field experience, so we were good friends for many years, worked together for a few years and I took over the business with my wife in 1985.

What about Kentucky makes it a good place for growing trees?
From the standpoint of the climate here, it's really ideal for trees—it's the habit and climate that they like. Trees are what would be here if people weren't here; it would be mostly deciduous trees growing, and a lot of

them would be nut trees. Mostly what we grow are native trees that are found in the area. Kentucky is almost central to the range of a lot of the trees we grow.

In addition to hickory trees, what other native Kentucky trees do you sell?
We do black walnuts, butternuts, heartnuts, chestnuts, pecans—things like that.

What does it take to grow a hickory orchard?
They're not quite as spreading as a big oak tree, but they get pretty tall—about sixty or seventy feet—and they spread out about twenty or thirty feet on the sides. Typically, you need two different, unrelated trees for cross-pollination. If there are wild hickory trees in the area, that wouldn't be a concern, or if your neighbors have hickories, but a lot of times in the suburbs, a hickory tree is hard to come by. Pollination is one of the major concerns for nut growers because you want to have good pollination, and typically nuts are not self-pollinating. Either the pollen is released before the little nutlet is ready, or the nutlet is ready far before the pollen is released, so with a single tree you're not going to get a lot of nuts grown. I would probably go with a couple of trees.

Describe the taste of a hickory nut.
It's a sweet flavor, very high quality, something like a pecan. Pecans are also hickories; they're all the same genus. Some are sweeter than others, but in general a hickory nut is like a very sweet pecan.

What's the difference between shagbark and shellbark trees?
They are two different species of hickory tree. The shellbark hickory nuts are sometimes called "king nuts" and are at least an inch and a half, maybe two inches, in diameter. They typically grow in bottoms along rivers and in open areas, and while you can find them occasionally in higher areas, they tend to be in the lowlands. They are very disease resistant; they don't really have any problem with fungus or scab on the leaves, anything like that. That is probably because they grow in the bottoms, where it's humid. They are a little bit thicker shell than the shagbark hickory nuts. The shagbarks are typically an upland species, probably a little bit more widely found than the shellbark hickories. The shellbark hickories were cut out of the bottoms because they were good to use for firewood but also because along the rivers had the best fields for crops. They were the first places cleared, so a lot of the

shellbark hickories were cut out years ago and are a little bit harder to find. Shagbarks, though, are found in the hillier ground and more widespread in the woods. They are pretty pervasive and tend to have a smaller nut with a thinner shell. They both have kind of a peeling, flaking bark that's similar and gives them a nice ornamental picture or appearance.

Would you recommend picking nuts in the wild? If so, what should folks look for in a good nut?

One of the main things to think about with hickory nuts is that there are actually several different species other than the shagbark and the shellbark, like pignut hickory and bitternut hickory. One of the first things to do when you pick them up is to crack a nut or crack a few nuts and make sure the nuts are full. Sometimes they might not have pollinated well, they might not be full or they might have weevils. Weevils are the biggest problem for nut trees and probably for fruit trees too—there's a weevil for every fruit or nut. The weevils that you find in hickories are similar to those you see in acorns. You can see the exit hole where the little worm comes out. Sometimes, you pick up nuts, and they look good, then you let them sit for a while and the eggs are in there and they hatch and come out, so make sure you think about that when you're picking up nuts. It's definitely important to make sure you're not picking up a bunch of nuts full of weevils or that aren't filled. With black walnuts, which are also good in sweets, that's not so much of a problem. They get little husk maggots who get in the green husks on the outside of the shell, but there's not much that gets into the meat of the black walnut, which makes them pretty easy to go pick up in the wild and get the nuts out of them. It's a little bit harder to get hickory nut kernels out of the trees in the wild because they haven't been selected for the nuts the way that grafted trees are selected.

What's your favorite dish to make with hickory nuts?

Well, I think hickory nut pie is pretty hard to beat. It's about the best. You can really eat them in anything you make with pecans or any other type of nut. They're very high-quality nuts, so they are also very good in cookies.

Are any types of hickory nuts rare?

We're looking for any trees that produce hickory nuts with exceptional cracking qualities. Not a lot of people are looking, but among those of us who are, that's what we're really going for. One of the hopes is that there's always a better nut out there to be found, and it's a continuing effort. This year, I heard about a real fine hickory up in Iowa with a really thin shell that may be good or better than most of the others that have been found, so that's encouraging. The problem is that most hickory nuts don't crack out that well. Most of them have the inner shell convoluted to where the kernel is held tightly inside, so when it's cracked, you get small pieces instead of a whole nut. Typically, a smooth inner shell identifies that the kernel will come clean when you crack the nut.

There aren't too many people who are working with hickory trees, but for me, they're about the most fulfilling thing to work with. I love how much diversity there is within the species and how the buds look distinct. For example, you look at a black walnut tree, and they pretty much look the same from one tree to another. If you look at a hickory tree, you can tell that they are individuals, that they are all different. It takes a while for them to mature and produce fruit, but when they do, it's hard to beat hickories.

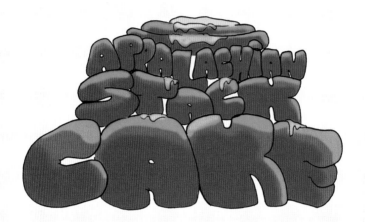

APPALACHIAN STACK CAKE

The Appalachian Stack Cake is far and away the dessert with the greatest association to the mountain region and is perhaps one of the most rustic confections still eaten today. Known for its spicy, none-too-sweet taste and thick, dense texture (more akin to a thick ginger biscuit than anything from Duncan Hines), the cake was said to have been carried along the Wilderness Trail by explorer James Harrod, the namesake of Harrodsburg, Kentucky, and a contemporary of Daniel Boone's.

Stack Cake Aliases
apple stack cake,
Confederate old-
fashioned stack cake,
apple washday cake

TRADITION SPOTLIGHT: PRESERVING TECHNIQUES

In addition to canning, pickling and candying, a method of preserving foods often used in Appalachia is drying. The drying of apples is particularly important for making stack cakes, as these dried apples are then either spiced in their dry form or rehydrated to constitute the gingery, tart filling between cake layers. In any of the drying preparations, the apples are cored and cut into the kind of wedges one would associate with an after-school snack (about 2 inches in diameter). Dried apples will more often than not turn brown, be quite wrinkly and have a rubbery texture and a tough, chewy bite much like a fruit leather or fruit jerky.

All fruits and vegetables used for drying should be well ripened, as immature fruit will have a sour taste and overly ripened fruit will produce mushy dried delicacies. In terms of measurements, six pounds of freshly picked apples will yield about one and a half pints of dried apples.

Drying the Old-Fashioned Way: The majority of the methods used by Appalachians in decades and centuries past relied on the outdoors, sun and time to properly dehydrate their fruits and vegetables. Apples were either laid out on long benches draped in muslin or placed on baking sheets and covered with cheesecloth or a thin fabric to keep bugs from disrupting the drying process. The process was significantly sped up by placing the apples in a place that received a good deal of constant, direct sunlight throughout the day.

Fruits and vegetables—including cucumbers, carrots and green beans—were also dehydrated by stringing them up in a kind of garland using a needle and thick thread. These were then placed along wash lines or in sunny kitchen windows to dry.

Drying in Modern Day: Food dehydrators are obviously the fastest and most effective choice for Appalachian families today to dry out their apples. Another well-tested method is using the oven on a low-heat setting (about 140°F) to sap all the liquid out of the fruit—a process that takes hours instead of several days like the outdoor methods. The use of a drying rack is an added boon that will increase the circulation of air and ensure that drying is even. Turning the apples and rotating pans during the drying process will speed it up significantly.

Popular Fruits and Vegetables to Dry: peaches, apples, pears, green beans, carrots, cucumbers

CULTURAL SPOTLIGHT: APPALACHIAN WEDDINGS

Move over, buttercream and tiny bride and groom figures. Stack cakes are the original wedding cakes of Appalachia. On the day of a wedding, community members and guests attending the ceremony would each make and bring a cake layer to stack for the bride's cake, which usually began with two to three layers. The mother and grandmother of the bride would receive the cake layers, spreading the dried apple mixture between the layers to sweeten it. The taller the cake ended up being, the more popular the bride. While some cakes would reach as tall as fourteen layers, the average height for a cake was in the six- to eight-layer range. The importance of togetherness and support in the mountain communities is reinforced by this cake, and the financial strain of an elaborate, multi-tiered wedding cake is removed.

Another Appalachian wedding tradition that has been less well preserved over the years is shivaree (also called serenading, belling or horning). After the wedding finished, most Appalachian couples did not have the money for a honeymoon, so they stayed in their own homes or inns nearby. The newlyweds' first night together, friends and family would gather to tease the couple by clanging pots and pans, shouting, singing or even carrying the new bride around town in a bathtub.

SIDEKICK COCKTAIL
SPIKED APPLE CIDER

Yield: 1 cocktail

2 ounces bourbon
5 ounces hot apple cider
¼ teaspoon cinnamon
¼ teaspoon ground nutmeg

Pour the bourbon into a tumbler (or mug, if you're feeling serious). Top up with apple cider and spices. Stir gently.

SIDEKICK RECIPE
WASHDAY CAKE

Another theory is that stack cakes were made primarily as "washday" cakes—a dessert that was typically made and assembled on Monday and then left to sit until Wednesday, when it was eaten during the hectic "washday" schedule. Here is another, more buttery version of the wash cake.

Yield: 1 9x9-inch cake
Active Time: 10 minutes * Total Time: 40 minutes

½ cup butter
1½ cups dark brown sugar
2 cups flour
1 cup buttermilk

1 teaspoon baking soda
1 large egg, beaten
1 teaspoon vanilla extract

Preheat oven to 350°F and grease baking dish. In a large bowl, using an electric handheld mixer, cream butter and sugar together until light and fluffy. Slowly add in flour and beat on medium speed until crumbly. Set aside. In a medium bowl, combine milk, baking soda, egg and vanilla. Add wet ingredients into dry ingredients and stir using a wooden spoon until combined. Bake until golden brown, about 30 minutes.

TIPS AND TRICKS

Cutting Corners: While the cake can be quite tedious to make, and some people cut corners by simply using an applesauce or apple butter filling between the layers, don't do it. The texture, taste and structure of the cake is made by the dried apple filling.

Let It Rest: It's important to let the cake rest—perhaps for one day, maybe two—before eating so that all the flavors are given time to intermingle. While some older recipes call for eating the cake warm, on the day of baking, it's probably because it was difficult to store the cake and keep it from bugs, rodents and grabby kid hands in generations past.

Castaway: The cast-iron skillet is the official cooking tool of Appalachia and the original vessel for cooking the layers of the stack cake. If you decide to go the traditional route for the cake, brush the cast-iron skillet generously with butter prior to each use. Most folks don't have more than one cast-iron skillet, so you're in luck: feel free to refill the skillet with batter immediately after one cake layer is finished and cook again. If you don't have one of these heavy, hand-me-down beauties, get one right away.

Appalachian Stack Cake

Yield: 1 7-layer, 9-inch stack cake
Active Time: 2 hours * Total Time: 5 hours
Special Tools: cast-iron skillet (optional)

½ cup unsalted butter, room temperature
1 cup dark brown sugar
1 large egg, beaten
½ cup sorghum syrup
½ cup buttermilk
6 cups all-purpose flour
½ teaspoon baking soda
1 teaspoon baking powder
¼ teaspoon salt
½ teaspoon nutmeg
1 teaspoon ground ginger
1½ teaspoons vanilla extract
cooked dried apples (see following recipe)

Preheat oven to 350°F and brush cake pan generously with butter. If making more than one cake layer at a time (dough makes seven layers), brush all pans with butter. Using a handheld electric mixer, cream together butter and sugar until light and fluffy. Add beaten egg, sorghum and buttermilk, beating on medium speed until completely combined. Set aside.

Sift flour, baking soda, baking powder, salt, nutmeg and ginger into a big mixing bowl. Make a well in center of dry ingredients and pour in wet mixture, beating on low until blended. Fold in vanilla extract. On a lightly floured surface, roll out dough until 1 inch thick. Using a pastry cutter, cut dough to fit in cake pan. Bake until browned, about 12 minutes.

When cool, layer cake with the cooked dried apple filling. Spread filling generously and evenly between layers. Slice cake into thin portions and immediately serve, if necessary, or let the flavors marry overnight before slicing for a more flavorful cake. The cake can keep, stored in an airtight container, for up to 5 days.

Cooked Dried Apples

2 cups dried apples
4 cups cold water
2 cups dark brown sugar
1 tablespoon sorghum
1 teaspoon allspice
1 teaspoon cinnamon
1 teaspoon nutmeg
1½ teaspoons cloves

Place apples in heavy-bottom pot and cover with cold water. Bring to a boil, then continue to cook over medium heat until apples begin to plump, about 20 minutes. Drain apples and place in a large bowl. Mash lightly with sugar and spices until completely coated. Allow to rest for 2 hours or overnight.

Blackberry Cobbler

Although it is not a fashionable pie for company,
[cobbler] *is very excellent for family use.*

—*Lettice Bryan*, The Kentucky Housewife *(1839)*

A juicy treat, the blackberry is one of the few fruits used with equal zest from Paducah to Pikeville, where it is baked into cakes, crafted into jams and makes the perfect addition to any sweet confection one's heart could desire. Don't pick them after the autumn season begins, though: many older generations in Appalachia still hold the old English belief that it's bad luck to eat blackberries picked in the fall because the devil has spit on them. While it may not be devil's expectorate, there is a higher probability that berries picked this late in the growing season will have mold, fungus or other unsavory diseases—so even if it's not Lucifer himself, it's probably best to stay away.

Blackberries in Song

"Garfield's Blackberry Blossom" by Lyle Lovett
"Blackberry Stone" by Laura Marling
"Blackberry Brandy" by T Bird & the Breaks

SWEET SPOTLIGHT:
COBBLER VERSUS BUCKLE VERSUS CRISP

The humble and delicious cobbler is a dessert that goes by many times, but it is often confused with its kissing cousins from other geographic locales. While the various branches of the cobbler tree have many similarities, their differences are enough to ensure that no one would call them by the wrong name at a family reunion.

In a blackberry cobbler, the berries are typically encrusted in a type of deep-dish fruit potpie. The crust, usually fluffy and biscuit style, is laid in a thick layer over the fruit, either as a single sheet of dough or cut into rounds ("cobbles"). In many places, a layer of biscuit dough is placed on both the top and the bottom of the fruit in order to sandwich the filling.

In a blackberry crisp, the fruit is sprinkled with a streusel-style topping of butter, sugar and flour. Often, especially in the fall or winter, diced nuts and oats are added to the crumb topping as well.

In a blackberry buckle, the fruit is gently folded into a prepared cake batter. The cake "buckles" around the fruit as it bakes, which creates small pockets in the final dessert. If the dish is to be served at an event, it is covered with a streusel-like topping.

In a blackberry grunt, the dish is prepared on the stovetop in a skillet, with the berries sitting atop a layer of thin, pie-like dough. The name is derived from the popping and gurgling sound the berries make as they stew.

TIPS AND TRICKS

The Berry Best: When picking blackberries, it's imperative to select those that are in their prime for the sweetest, most flavorful dishes possible. Blackberries develop differently than most other fruits, and even blackberries that might look mature to the untrained eye can be misleading (this rule can also be applied to many men).

When blackberries are unripe, instead of being a green or yellow color, they are a ruby red. (The old Appalachian words of warning, "Blackberries are red when they're green," is a good mantra to keep in the back of your mind.) Instead, wait until the berries are full, juicy and a deep purple (almost black) hue before picking. Unripened blackberries will not continue to ripen after being picked, so timing is critical to gathering the sweetest berries possible.

Ensuring that the plants themselves are healthy is equally as important. Blackberry plants that have turned a burnt orange color should be uprooted immediately or avoided while picking, as it is the indicator of serious fungal diseases.

Fun Fact
The blackberry was designated the official state fruit of Kentucky in 2004.

Blackberry Aliases
bramble fruit, black raspberries, black caps, dew berries, thimble berries

Cobbler Aliases
pandowdy, grunt, slump, buckle, crisp, bird's nest pudding

SIDEKICK COCKTAIL
BLACKBERRY SMASH

Yield: 6 servings

1 cup blackberries
6 ounces gin
1 ounce freshly squeezed orange juice
1 ounce simple syrup
dash of orange bitters

Muddle blackberries in a small bowl. Combine with gin and let macerate at room temperature for 1 hour. Using a blender, blend the blackberries and gin until smooth, about 20 seconds. Strain the mixture into a small bowl and add orange juice, simple syrup and orange bitters, stirring until combined. Fill six cocktail glasses one-third full with crushed ice, pour drink over and serve.

BLACKBERRY COBBLER

Yield: 1 8x8-inch casserole dish (8–10 servings)
Active Time: 15 minutes * Total Time: 1 hour, 15 minutes
Special Tools: casserole dish

4 cups fresh blackberries, washed and patted dry

4 tablespoons dark brown sugar

$^2/_3$ cup plus 4 tablespoons flour

$^1/_2$ cup granulated sugar

$^2/_3$ teaspoon baking powder

$^1/_2$ teaspoon salt

2 large eggs, room temperature

4 tablespoons buttermilk

1 teaspoon vanilla extract

10 tablespoons unsalted butter, melted

Preheat oven to 350°F. Grease your baking dish with butter, coat with flour and set aside. In a small mixing bowl, combine the blackberries and brown sugar until berries are thoroughly coated. Line the bottom of the baking dish with berries.

In a medium bowl, sift together flour, granulated sugar, baking powder and salt. Stir in the eggs, followed by buttermilk and vanilla extract until combined, then add melted butter. The batter should be thick and oozy—the kind that you wanted to lick off the back of a spoon as a kid.

Pour the batter over the berries, making sure that it is evenly distributed. Bake for 50 minutes to 1 hour, or until the edges begin to crisp and brown. Allow to cool for 1 hour, slice and serve with ice cream. The cobbler can be kept up to three days stored in the refrigerator, but you probably won't be able to keep it around that long.

*E*ven for those of us with mild mountain accents, there is a tendency to accidentally slip an *r* into words where it doesn't belong—especially when we're excited about something (or mad, but you really don't want to see one of us mad). This is particularly true for one of the region's favorite native gourds, the cushaw, which is frequently referred to as the "cershaw" by folks eagerly discussing what delicious treats they will be making with it. This crook-neck, green striped vegetable is not only a staple of holiday meals and a perfect substitute for pumpkin in most dishes but also the inspiration for one of the region's greatest phrases. "Your head is as hard as a cushaw!" means that someone is being particularly stubborn or unnecessarily difficult about a situation; it is frequently heard being yelled at husbands by their wives.

CARTOON CUSHAW: THE SHMOO

Aside from the comic strip being one of the twentieth century's most brilliant tongue-in-cheek satires of western civilization, the *Lil' Abner* mid-twentieth-century sensation the Shmoo, created by legendary cartoonist Al Capps, was rumored to have been modeled after the shape of a cushaw.

SIDEKICK RECIPE CUSHAW BUTTER

Yield: 6 pints
Active Time: 10 minutes
Total Time: 2 hours, 40 minutes

4½ cups pureed cushaw
¼ cup apple cider
1 cup light brown sugar
4 tablespoons sorghum
2 tablespoons ground cinnamon
1 teaspoon ground ginger
1 teaspoon vanilla extract
1 teaspoon lemon juice

Cushaw Pronunciation
coo-shaw (*coo*, as in the sound a baby makes, and *shaw*, as in the classic Morgan Freeman movie *Shawshank Redemption*)

Cushaw Aliases
southern sweet potato squash, crookneck squash, kershaw squash

Combine all ingredients in heavy-bottom saucepan over medium heat. Cook uncovered, reducing the mixture and stirring occasionally to keep from burning, for 30 minutes. Cover with a lid and cook for 1–2 hours, stirring every 20 minutes with a wooden spoon. The butter is ready when the mixture coats the back of a spoon. Serve immediately; store in the refrigerator for up to two weeks or the freezer for up to three months.

TIPS AND TRICKS

Cushaw Cutting: Using a well-sharpened paring knife, very carefully slice off the neck of the squash, separating it from the rotund body. Slice the neck into 1½- to 2-inch pieces, discarding the end piece from the top of the neck. Slice away the outer green rind of the cushaw, leaving only the pale yellow flesh of the vegetable. Moving your attention to the cushaw body, divide it down the center vertically into two halves. Take a butter knife or grapefruit spoon and circle the edges of the pulpy center to jiggle loose the insides. Using a large spoon, an ice cream scoop or a melon baller, scoop out the seeds and pulp and discard (alternatively, save the seeds and roast them with cinnamon and sugar, much like pumpkin seeds, or plant them to form your own cushaw empire).

Working with one half at a time, slice the body into crescent-shaped, 2-inch slices. (These slices will end up resembling a cut-up cantaloupe.) Using a paring knife, strip the striped outer rind of the cushaw from the inside flesh and toss the rind.

Preserving Puree: Cushaw puree can be frozen in airtight containers for up to three months. If you go the canning route, the puree can live happily and healthily for upward of a year.

Pain in the Neck: The neck tends to be the toughest part of the cushaw. When roasting the vegetable for puree, begin cooking the neck pieces about 10–15 minutes before the body pieces.

Retaining Water: Cushaws have a bit more water than traditional pumpkins, so in case you decide to get creative and switch out a cushaw for pumpkin in any additional recipes, cut the liquid in the recipe by at least one-fourth.

TIPS FOR GROWING CUSHAWS

Timing Is Everything: This hard-shelled winter squash is an ideal crop to grow in a climate where daytime temperatures average sixty-five degrees and there is at least a 120-day growing season.

Sprouting Up: Seeds sprout in 4 to 7 days, and squash is ready for harvest about 110 days from sowing.

Putting Down Roots: Seeds should be planted in late spring, one inch deep in mounds of soil (known as "hills"). Space seeds roughly five feet apart, with four to five seeds planted in each hill.

SIDEKICK RECIPE
CUSHAW BREAD

Yield: 1 9-inch loaf
Active Time: 30 minutes * Total Time: 1 hour, 40 minutes

1½ cups all-purpose flour

1 teaspoon baking powder

¼ teaspoon baking soda

¼ teaspoon salt

½ cup butter, softened

1 cup light brown sugar

2 large eggs

1 teaspoon vanilla extract

1 cup pureed cushaw

½ cup chocolate chips (optional)

Preheat oven to 350°F. Grease and flour loaf pan generously and set aside. Sift flour, baking powder, baking soda and salt into a medium bowl. In a large bowl, using a handheld electric mixer, cream butter and sugar until light and fluffy. Add the eggs, one at a time, blending after each addition, then fold in vanilla. Add cushaw (and chips if using) and mix to combine. Add dry ingredients ¼ of the mixture at a time to the wet ingredients, blending well after each addition. The finished batter will be thick and heavy. Pour into prepared pan and bake until a toothpick inserted in the center comes out clean, about 1 hour and 10 minutes.

SIDEKICK COCKTAIL
THE HARDHEADED CUSHAW

Yield: 1 cocktail

1 ounce cushaw puree

1 ounce dark rum

½ ounce spiced rum

dash of nutmeg

cinnamon stick

Combine first three ingredients in a chilled cocktail shaker filled with ice and shake for 15–20 seconds. Strain into a chilled lowball glass, garnish with nutmeg and cinnamon stick and serve.

CUSHAW PIE

Yield: 1 9-inch pie (8 servings)
Active Time: 30 minutes * Total Time: 1 hour, 30 minutes
Special Tools: pie plate, paring knife

For the Crust:
1 cup slivered almonds
1¼ cups all-purpose flour
12 tablespoons unsalted butter
3 tablespoons granulated sugar
1 tablespoon bourbon
3 to 4 tablespoons cold water

For the Filling:
3 large eggs, beaten
12 ounces evaporated milk
1 teaspoon vanilla
2 cups pureed cushaw
1 tablespoon unsalted butter, melted
⅔ cup light brown sugar
1 teaspoon ground cinnamon
½ teaspoon ground ginger
½ teaspoon salt
½ teaspoon allspice
½ teaspoon freshly ground nutmeg
¼ teaspoon ground cloves

For the Crust:

Place almonds, flour, butter and sugar in food processor and pulse until the mixture is crumbly, or 8 to 10 short pulses. While continuing to pulse, add the bourbon and then the water 1 tablespoon at a time until the dough begins to form a ball. Transfer to a sheet of plastic wrap and press into a ¼-inch-thick disc. Wrap tightly and refrigerate for at least 1 hour. Adjust oven rack to center position and preheat oven to 350°F. Remove dough from refrigerator. Using a rolling pin, roll dough into a circle roughly 12 inches in diameter. Transfer to a pie plate and trim edges. Line with foil, fill with pie weights and bake empty crust until golden brown, about 10 minutes. Remove from oven, remove weights and set aside.

For the Filling:

In a small bowl, combine eggs, evaporated milk and vanilla and blend with a wooden spoon until smooth. In a large bowl, combine squash, butter, sugar and spices, whisking until completely combined. Add milk mixture to squash mixture and fold together. Pour into prepared crust. Bake for an hour or until a toothpick inserted in the center comes out clean. Serve immediately or keep covered in the refrigerator for up to three days.

Well, I don't mind being an old gray grandpa /
If you'll be my gray grandma /
But I suggest we go have our milk and cookies /
In the shade of the old paw-paw.
—"Nothing But a Breeze," Jesse Winchester, 1977

We landed one time only to let the men gather pawpaws or the custard apple of
which this country abounds, and the men are very fond of.
—Meriwether Lewis, September 15, 1806

Pawpaws are something of an agricultural mystery. The oblong, green fruit—sometimes likened to a big, green football—is native to eastern Kentucky, growing throughout Appalachia alongside more traditional fruit tree counterparts. The catch? Pawpaws are relatives of subtropical fruits that wouldn't last one temperature dip in the mountains. Their soft, supple inner flesh tastes like it deserves its own tiki drink and is the perfect fruit for your next taste testing adventure. (Also, I'm calling it right now: pawpaws will be a food trend in five years, so get in on the ground floor.)

SPOTLIGHT:
FORAGING IN KENTUCKY

Foraging has long been a means of gathering delicious and readily accessible foods in Kentucky, with an abundance of trees, bushes and shrubs growing produce just waiting to be plucked and picked up. Due to their soft nature, pawpaws fall to the ground when ripe, making them a perfect fruit for which to forage. In the spring, summer and fall, there are a limitless number of wonderful items for which to forage across the state:

Spring: morel mushrooms, ramps, sassafras, English nettles, dandelions

Summer: mulberries, blackberries, wild onion, hackberries

Fall: hickory nuts, black walnuts, crabapples, apples

A handy list of tips and tricks to keep you safe from illness and the environment green and lush when foraging includes:

When in Doubt, Don't
If you're unsure what a plant might be, it's probably best to leave it alone. First and foremost, it could potentially kill you, but also it might be endangered or the habitat for an endangered animal.

No Greedy Gut Magpies Allowed
Don't wipe out an entire blackberry bush or pick dozens upon dozens of mushrooms. It's polite to not take more than one-tenth of whatever you are harvesting. Mind your manners.

Aliases
Kentucky custard apple, Appalachian banana, poor man's banana, prairie banana

History Note
Papaws are the fruit credited with saving Lewis and Clark from starvation. The two men had run out of rations and were getting close to starving when they found a pawpaw patch, which sustained them for a good portion of their expedition.

SPOTLIGHT:
SECRET, NATIVE FRUIT TREES

Kentucky is the perfect climate for growing a wide variety of well-known fruit and nut trees, including pears, apples, wild cherry and American plum trees (staples of Cherokee Indian diets in the region prior to the settling of the state). The more interesting, and perhaps delicious, trees are the large number flying under the radar, including the pawpaw, that are native to the state and produce succulent fruits or provide ideal spicing for an after-dinner treat.

Common (American) Persimmon

While Asian persimmons tend to dominate the supermarket aisles, the common (or American) persimmon is a native Kentucky fruit that has gained a strong cult following in farmers' markets across the state. Persimmons have a bitter, astringent taste when unripe and require a long ripening period to reach their deep yellow or orange color. The ripened fruit is typically ready for harvest in the autumn, around October. If the fruit looks a little shriveled up and like it's past its prime, it's ready to go, with a taste that is similar to a nectarine or apricot.

PERSIMMON PUDDING
Yield: 10–12 servings
Active Time: 15 minutes * Total Time: 2 hours
Special Tools: 2 8x8-inch baking dishes

1 cup common persimmon pulp
¾ cup granulated sugar
4 tablespoons unsalted butter
1 large egg
1½ cups heavy cream
1 cup flour
1 teaspoon baking powder
¼ teaspoon baking soda
½ teaspoon ginger
½ teaspoon cinnamon
½ teaspoon allspice

Preheat oven to 350°F. Grease baking dishes with butter, dust with flour and set aside. In a large mixing bowl, using a handheld electric mixer, cream together pulp, sugar, butter, egg and heavy cream until smooth. Sift in flour, baking powder, baking soda, ginger, cinnamon and allspice, mixing on medium speed until combined. Pour the batter equally into the two baking dishes and bake in the oven until a toothpick comes out clean, about 1 hour. Don't be alarmed if the puddings fall when removed from the oven. Place pudding in refrigerator and allow to set up for 30–45 minutes. Serve immediately.

Downy Serviceberry

These rich, small red and deep purple berries—also called juneberries—grow in clusters on trees that are known for their lush, full white blossoms in the springtime. The berries only appear for several short weeks during the year and are also a favorite of cardinals and other regional birds. Those who wish to bake with them should be diligent in both battling away winged competitors and ensuring that the berries are the deepest hue possible before picking. The berries are slightly gritty and taste like blueberries when eaten raw, but they can be made into any number of desserts where they tend to dehydrate much like raisins.

SERVICEBERRY JAM
Yield: 2 mason jars
Active Time: 30 minutes * Total Time: 1 hour
Special Tools: mason jars

4 cups serviceberries
2 oranges
1½ cups water
½ cup lemon juice
3 cups sugar

In a large, heavy-bottom pot, boil jars to sterilize for 5 minutes. Set aside and allow to cool. In a food processor, add berries and pulse until coarsely chopped, about 10 seconds. Juice oranges and set aside in a small bowl. Using a zester, zest the oranges and add to heavy-bottom saucepan along with berries and water over high heat.

Bring to a boil, cooking until fruit is tender. Add juice from oranges, lemon juice and sugar. Boil 20 minutes or until the mixture is thick enough to coat the back of a spoon. Pour jam into jars and place jars back in boiling water for 10 minutes to sterilize. Remove carefully using tongs and store in a cool, dry place.

Elderberry

A small tree (or large shrub) that is a member of the honeysuckle family and native to the mountain regions of the state, elderberries grow in large, bulbous clusters that are a deep blue-purple color. It was thought for centuries in Appalachian folklore that growing elderberries outside of one's house was a highly effective way to ward off witches. While on their own elderberries are incredibly tart and not worth eating, they are easily made into a wide variety of syrups, jams, jellies and wine and are frequently mixed in with sweeter berries as a pie filling.

ELDERBERRY SYRUP

While this syrup is delicious on pancakes or waffles, it also is reputed to have the ability to treat the flu and ward off symptoms of a cold.

1 pound fresh elderberries, stems removed
1 cup white granulated sugar
$^1/_3$ cup clover honey
1 tablespoon cinnamon

In a large, heavy-bottom pot, boil jars to sterilize for 5 minutes. Wash berries, pat dry and place in a medium saucepan over low heat, muddling gently with a potato masher. Bring to a boil over medium heat, stirring often. When the berries are fully broken down, remove from heat and run through a food mill to separate juice from pulp and (very bitter) seeds. Place juice in a small saucepan and add sugar. Bring mixture to a low boil over medium heat, stirring occasionally, until mixture becomes frothy. Remove from heat. Bring water to a boil in a large, heavy-bottom pot. When cooled, fold in honey and cinnamon. Pour syrup into sterilized jars and secure lids. Process in boiling water for 5 minutes. Remove jars carefully using tongs and store in a cool, dry place.

Pawpaws in Song
"Way Down Yonder in the Pawpaw Patch"

While many people outside Appalachia have never laid eyes on a pawpaw, a well-known, catchy (and potentially irritatingly repetitive) children's song has given this hidden fruit a wider audience. Despite being aimed at children, the song is actually quite accurate in describing how pawpaws grow and are often collected. Pawpaws are most likely to grow in valleys or bottomland (hence, "down yonder") near rivers or other bodies of water. They also are not typically stand-alone trees, instead growing in small colonies, which are often referred to as patches.

Where oh where is dear little Nellie?
Where oh where is dear little Nellie?
Where oh where is dear little Nellie?
Way down yonder in the pawpaw patch

Come on, kids, let's go find her
Come on, kids, let's go find her
Come on, kids, let's go find her
Way down yonder in the pawpaw patch

Pickin' up paw paws,
Put 'em in your pocket
Pickin' up paw paws,
Put 'em in your pocket
Pickin' up paw paws,
Put 'em in your pocket
Way down yonder in the pawpaw patch

GINGER PAWPAW CUSTARD

Yield: 6–8 servings
Active Time: 10 minutes * Total Time: 1 hour
Special Tools: ramekins, 9x13-inch baking dish

2 cups heavy cream
¾ cup granulated sugar
3 large eggs, room temperature

½ teaspoon ginger powder
1 cup pawpaw puree
candied ginger, for garnish

Preheat oven to 325°F. In a small bowl, combine all ingredients and stir gently until incorporated. Pour custard into small, oven-safe ramekins or custard cups. Position ramekins in baking dish and fill dish halfway with boiling water, making sure not to add water to the custards. Bake until the custards set, about 50 minutes. Remove ramekins carefully from the oven, allow to cool, garnish with candied ginger and serve immediately.

PAWPAW ICE CREAM

Yield: 2 quarts
Active Time: 30 minutes * Total Time: 2 hours, 30 minutes
Special Tools: ice cream maker

2 cups heavy cream
3 large eggs
1 cup granulated sugar
¾ cup pawpaw puree

2 tablespoons bourbon
½ teaspoon vanilla extract
5–6 dashes orange bitters

Using a double boiler, or a large metal bowl sitting on top of gently boiling water, heat cream, reserving ½ cup. In a medium bowl, combine eggs, sugar and remaining milk. In a steady stream, add egg mixture slowly to hot milk, stirring constantly to avoid burning or overcooking. Custard is ready when it is thick enough to coat the back of a spoon. Remove custard from heat, allowing it to cool to room temperature. Once custard has reached room temperature, fold in pawpaw puree, bourbon, vanilla and orange bitters. Pour mixture into ice cream machine and freeze according to the manufacturer's instructions.

PAWPAW BREAD

Yield: 2 8-inch loaves

Active Time: 20 minutes * Total Time: 1 hour, 20 minutes

For the Bread:
1/3 cup unsalted butter
2/3 cup light brown sugar
2 large eggs
1 cup pawpaw puree
1¾ cups all-purpose flour
2 teaspoons baking powder
¼ teaspoon baking soda
½ cup golden raisins

For the Frosting:
1 teaspoon orange zest, grated
½ cup unsalted butter
1 tablespoon fresh orange juice
1 pound confectioners' sugar
6 tablespoons heavy cream

For the Bread:

Preheat oven to 350°F. Generously grease loaf pans and dust with flour. Set aside. Using an electric handheld mixer, cream butter, slowly adding sugar until light and fluffy. Add eggs, one at a time, beating well after each addition. Beat in pawpaw puree. Sift remaining dry ingredients into a large bowl and add to butter mixture ¼ at a time, beating until smooth after each addition. Fold in raisins. Pour batter into loaf pans and bake until a toothpick inserted into the loaf comes out clean, about 1 hour.

For the Frosting:

Zest orange using a zester and set aside. Using a handheld electric mixer in a medium bowl, cream butter until light and fluffy. Fold in orange juice and zest using a wooden spoon. Add confectioners' sugar alternately with cream, beginning and ending with sugar, until frosting is thick and spreadable. Once bread has cooled, spread frosting on top and allow to set for 1–2 hours. Once frosting is firm, serve immediately or cover and store in an airtight container.

SWEET SOUND OFF:
SHERRI CRABTREE
KSU PAWPAW RESEARCH

Kentucky State University in Frankfort has become the mecca for all pawpaw research in the United States, leading the way in not only developing and promoting Kentucky's ugly duckling fruit but also researching ways to make it more popular nationally.

Where in Kentucky are you from? Where did you go to school?
I grew up in Bowling Green, Kentucky, then went to the University of Kentucky, where I got my bachelor's and master's in horticulture. I've been working at Kentucky State University researching pawpaws ever since I graduated, so about thirteen years now.

How did you get into pawpaw research?
I was always interested in fruit crops in particular, and being a unique fruit crop, I was interested in working with pawpaws. It's really interesting to me, this native fruit that's not quite as well known as other fruits.

How did Kentucky State University [located in Frankfort, Kentucky] *become the center for pawpaw research in the country?*
Pawpaw research at KSU started in the early 1990s under Professor Brett Callaway, then Kirk Pomper took over the research program in 1998, so I've been working for him my entire time here.

What kind of work do you all do on a daily basis?
The main thing we're working on right now is cultivar* development and evaluation. We have thousands of trees that are seedlings that people have sent us from all around the United States, all around the native range of pawpaws, so we looked at those to see if any of them have potential as new varieties or cultivars. We also have a small breeding program and will do crosses that are good to hopefully come up with new pawpaw varieties. We test them to see how well they grow in Kentucky; growers have trials at their sites also to see how they do out in the real world as well. We've named and released one cultivar from KSU, so hopefully we'll be naming and releasing a few more cultivars for commercial purposes soon. We're getting more into process and value-added products because the fresh fruit has such a short

shelf life. We're looking at how to best handle the fruit, how to process it for freezing and looking at products that would be good to make with the frozen pawpaw pulp—ice cream is really popular and we've been working with a jam maker this year. We're also working with area restaurants and winemakers to try and get pawpaw products on the menu [at] various places.

A cultivar is a plant or grouping of plants selected for desirable characteristics that can be maintained by propagation.

What's it been like to work with restaurants and winemakers? Are they receptive to pawpaws?
Yes! There are several restaurants and chefs who are interested in local foods and heritage recipes—items that were popular in Appalachia but aren't quite as well known now. Jonathan's at Gratz Park in Lexington has worked with pawpaw in the past, and there are a couple of restaurants in Louisville—Limestone and Seviche—who are doing some pawpaw items now.

We're also working with Wildside Winery in Versailles, and Rising Sun Vineyard in Lawrenceburg got some pawpaws this year to make a pawpaw wine. They made a very successful jam for us in the past. There's also a jam maker in Corbin who we've worked with to develop a pawpaw jam recipe.

What does pawpaw wine taste like?
It's really good, but it makes a pretty sweet wine—kind of like a dessert wine. It's a golden color and sugary, perfect for after meals.

Describe the pawpaw tree, how it grows, where it grows, etc.
The pawpaw tree is really a small tree and doesn't get over fifteen to twenty feet tall. In the wild, it's part of the forest understory, so it's along river bottoms and in stream banks. It will form "patches" because the trees send up root suckers, so there will be these huge pawpaw patches in the woods that are all basically from one genotype or a single mother tree that sent up shoots from the roots. This is how they are able to form big patches and spread. They do have to cross-pollinate, and that's why in wild patches you often won't see many fruit, because they all may be connected to the same mother tree. They grow well in full sun, so if people are so inclined, they can grow them in orchards and backyards in full sun just like an apple tree. Growers would just need to get two different seedlings or two different varieties to cross-pollinate and produce fruit.

Pawpaws actually are often likened to tropical fruit. How would you describe the taste?
I usually describe the taste as a mango-banana blend. Different varieties of pawpaws have different tastes and undertones, kind of like how different apples will taste slightly different. There are some pawpaws that have more of a pineapple flavor, some have more of a cantaloupe flavor [and] some have a sort of caramel, coffee flavor. The flesh is custardy, like an avocado. The rest of the family is all tropical fruits. There are relatives of pawpaws found in South America, Central America and Florida like custard apples, sweetsop and cherimoya. They have a similar flavor but are only found in the tropics or subtropics. The pawpaw is so unique, then, because it tastes tropical [and] comes from a tropical family but grows wild in Kentucky.

How many different kinds of pawpaw trees are there?
There are about fifty cultivars of pawpaws available, so quite a few, but only about thirty available commonly.

Pawpaws are generally not very pretty. Could you describe what one looks like?
The fruit itself we often describes as looking like a "green potato," and they average about a half pound in size, four to six inches long. They have a green skin, and the skin doesn't change color when it ripens. Most of them don't turn yellow when they ripen, though some will get a hint of yellow; most remain green. Sometimes, you'll see a hint of brown or brown spots on the fruit. It's a fungal infection that's really just cosmetic and doesn't damage the fruit. Pawpaws are very soft, so you might see other blotches or blemishes on the skin from sun scald or damages from branches. It's just a funny green fruit.

Pawpaw flowers also aren't very good looking, either. Could you describe what they look like?
They are pretty small and kind of reddish-brownish. Pawpaws are pollinated by flies, not by bees like most flowers. You can kind of see how the flower looks a little "meat-like" in order to attract the flies. A lot of people are afraid that they smell bad, but they don't really—they have kind of a musky scent to them.

Talk about shelf life for pawpaws. Is this one of the main reasons that they haven't seen more commercial success?
Pawpaws have a really short shelf life when they are ripe. The fruit, when it's totally ripe, has only about a two-day—three-day max—shelf life. It also bruises very easily, so it's hard to pick them, store them and ship them

effectively. They can be picked a little bit under ripe; you can't pick them rock hard or they'll never ripen, but if you pick them when they barely start to soften, they can keep for a couple of weeks in the refrigerator and you can pull them out whenever you want them to continue to ripen.

Is the pulp easy to freeze?

Yes, it is, and that's really the best way to store it. Pawpaw pulp is really best, in my opinion, not cooked—when it's cooked, it can get a little bit of a brownish color to it, so freezing it raw is the best way to store it. We use a food mill to remove the skin and puree it up and put the fresh, raw pulp in freezer bags. It will keep that way for a year or two.

Which celebrity is the pawpaw most like?

Maybe someone kind of wacky like Russell Brand? Not that attractive but with their own kind of appeal—definitely not mainstream.

What was your first thought when you ate a pawpaw?

I thought it was a really rich fruit, rich and sweet, and I was very surprised that something so tropical was growing wild in Kentucky. Also that it wasn't better known because it has a really nice flavor to it. I didn't grow up eating them, though.

What is your favorite dish to make with pawpaws?

I think ice cream is really the best use for pawpaws, aside from eating them raw. You can use it in any recipe that would call for bananas, but I think it's really best when it's uncooked, so something like ice cream or smoothies. We also have experimented with crème brûlée and custards that have turned out really nicely.

When you have boiled in this manner as many apples as you wish, put the whole of them in a large kettle, or kettles, with the cider, and simmer it over a bed of coals till it is so thick, that it is with some difficulty you can stir it: it should be stirred almost constantly, with a wooden spaddle, or paddle, or it will be certain to scorch at the bottom or sides of the kettle. Shortly before you take it from the fire, season it as before directed, and then put it up in jars.

—*Lettice Bryan,* The Kentucky Housewife *(1839)*

HISTORY LESSON: COPPER KETTLES AND WOODEN PADDLES

Apple butter was far more than a delicious spread for generations past—it was an opportunity for families and friends to gather and celebrate the harvest, autumn and the bounty that it brings. Apple butter is traditionally simmered outdoors in large, forty-gallon copper kettles over an open fire of woods or coals in a clearing near a family member's house. The process—which usually took place on a Saturday—was an all-day affair that required constant attention and stirring with a long-handled wooden spatula from the women and men who gathered to help the apple butter cook. Women typically assumed most of the responsibility for overseeing and  stirring the apple butter, which had to keep moving constantly in order not to stick and burn. About 10–12 bushels per kettle were typical for forty-gallon copper kettles.

INGREDIENT SPOTLIGHT: APPLES

Tradition holds that the best apples for making apple butter are those that are inherently sweet, have a juicy bite to them and are soft enough to ensure they will cook down quickly. However, many people prefer a little bit of pucker to their apple butter, which is all the more reason to include some diversity when picking your apples for butter-making. Here are some solid options.

Jonathan: This green-and-red mottled apple is quite sugary, crisp and one of the primary apples preferred for making apple butter.

Winesap: A pale pink-and-yellow apple known for its fragrant, almost wine-like aroma, which adds an interesting depth of flavor to apple butter.

Braeburn: A light-red apple with orange and yellow streaks, this fairly large apple has less liquid than many others, making it a good choice for thickening the apple butter.

Cortland: With its small size, soft texture and sweet, succulent taste, this is one of the best apples if you're in need of a traditionally sweet, quick-cooking apple butter.

Jonagold: This hybrid between the Jonathan and the Golden Delicious has a crisp, sweet-tart taste to it and is rather large in size.

SPOTLIGHT EVENT:
THE KENTUCKY APPLE FESTIVAL, PAINTSVILLE, KENTUCKY

Apples have a prized place in Kentucky's culinary heritage, and each October, the town of Paintsville attracts enthusiasts and hungry mouths from across the state to its weekend-long festival dedicated to the crunchy fruit. For fifty-one years, the festival has been home to an abundance of apple treats—fried apple pies, cakes and sauces—and an annual parade with floats, bands and a royal court all dedicated to the apple theme.

TIPS AND TRICKS

Color Theory: If you can't tell if your apple butter is done, look at the color: when it is still in its applesauce form, the mixture will be a yellow or light pink color. When it's in its true apple butter state, the mixture will be a dark, rich brown or burgundy shade.

Thin Is In: If the apple butter seems too thick once cooled, it can be easily thinned with apple cider.

Don't You Cry: One way to tell that the apple butter is done cooking is that it has stopped "weeping"—another name for the water separating from the pulp of the apples.

Sugar on My Tongue: When your apple butter looks ready to roll, it might seem almost too sweet to the taste when you put it in your mouth still warm. No worries. This phenomenon occurs because hot items taste naturally sweeter than cool items to our taste buds. The flavors will even out when the apple butter cools.

Oh, Honey: Trying to go all-natural? Apple butter can also be sweetened with honey.

All Dried Out: Apple butter can also easily be made with dried apples, which have a very condensed and intense flavor, or a blend of fresh apples and dried apples.

SIDEKICK RECIPE
APPLE BUTTER PIE WITH OATMEAL PECAN CRUST

Yield: 1 9-inch pie
Active Time: 30 minutes * Total Time: 1 hour, 30 minutes

For the Crust:
2 cups rolled oats
1 cup all-purpose flour
2 teaspoons cinnamon
½ cup pecans, chopped
¼ cup dark brown sugar
1 teaspoon vanilla extract
1 cup butter, melted

For the Filling:
1 cup apple butter
½ cup dark brown sugar
1 medium egg
1 teaspoon all-purpose flour
1½ cups sweetened condensed milk

For the Crust:
Mix oats, flour, cinnamon, pecans, sugar and vanilla together in a large bowl. Pour melted butter over mixture and stir until completely combined. Press mixture into bottom and sides of pie plate (it will be a thick crust) and refrigerate until ready to use.

For the Filling:
Adjust oven rack to center position and preheat oven to 350°F. Whisk all ingredients in a bowl until well combined. Pour into prepared pie crust. Bake until crust is golden and a toothpick inserted in the center comes out clean, about 40 minutes.

APPLE BUTTER

Yield: 3 pints
Active Time: 30 minutes * Total Time: 2 hours

12–15 apples, peeled, sliced and cored
1 cup unfiltered apple cider
½ cup dark brown sugar
1½ tablespoons cinnamon
1 teaspoon cloves
1 teaspoon allspice
1½ teaspoons ginger
½ teaspoon lemon juice

Combine apples and apple cider in a large heavy-bottom pot over low heat. Cook mixture, stirring occasionally, until the apples begin to fall apart, about 1 hour. Using an immersion blender, puree apples until smooth but still chunky. Stir in sugar, spices and lemon juice. Continue cooking over low heat, stirring occasionally to keep it from burning, until the mixture thickens. The apple butter is ready when a smear of it onto a cutting board doesn't "weep" or separate the apple puree from the water, about an additional 2 hours, depending on the apples. Let cool and eat immediately or store in the refrigerator for a week or freeze for up to a year.

Slow Cooker Apple Butter

Yield: 5 pints

25–30 apples*
2½ teaspoons cinnamon
I teaspoon allspice
I½ teaspoons ground cloves
I teaspoon ginger
½ teaspoon lemon juice
2–3 cups granulated sugar

Core and cut the apples into 2-inch slices and fill slow cooker until at capacity. Add spices, lemon juice and sugar, stir until combined and set the slow cooker on low heat for IO hours, stirring intermittently. After IO hours, repeat the process, adding new apples on top of the cooked-down apple mixture. Each time more apples are added, include the same amount of spices and sugar as in the original batch or to taste. If the apples don't seem to be cooking down quickly enough, vent the lid to help speed up the process.

Continue cooking until apple butter is the thickness you prefer—preferably thick enough to coat the back of a spoon. After the mixture is entirely cooked down, smooth out the consistency if necessary using a food mill or immersion blender. Let cool and eat immediately or store in the refrigerator for a week or freeze for up to a year.

*see "Spotlight" section for apple suggestions

Sweet Sound Off:
Terry Boyd
Boyd's Orchard, Versailles, Kentucky

With more than sixty acres of orchards and farmland in central Kentucky, Boyd's Orchard has become a destination location for apple picking and apple-themed confections. In addition to significant retail apple production, the menagerie of animals, activities and kid-friendly stimulation provided by the farm is a sure sign of its status as a leader in the wave of next-generation, entertainment-focused farms.

How did you start working with the orchard?

Well, we can go way back—I'm fifth generation doing fruit horticulture, apples, peaches and the like. All of those generations, and myself included, were all wholesale growers and not really retail as we are now. The structure was totally different. In the 1990s, the wholesale market for fruit went into the tank—not just in one spot but just as a general rule for a six- or eight-year period. It was incredibly difficult for that period of time to maneuver through it and make it work. A lot of us who are doing this agritourism or agritainment business came from that era when the wholesale times were hard. In order to diversify, and not fall flat on our face totally, we stepped outside the wholesale arena and tried to create some extra income from the farm that we weren't able to get in the wholesale business. The kickoff of the bad times in the 1990s was how most of us got started in these different avenues of promoting our farms and fruit like retailing fruit and preparing foods on the farm. We started actually back in the early 1990s. I could see the handwriting on the wall that wholesaling was not going to be something I could continue in and do successfully.

In 1993, we started looking for different properties where we could relocate from our original orchard in southern Illinois to expand the farm—we couldn't stay there because it was such a rural place it was never going to be really good because the population wasn't quite high enough, so we had limited potential. We ended up in the Versailles area ten years ago on a farm that was already an orchard, a place that was just retailing and wholesaling a little bit of product by itself. Even retailers can't get by just on fruit anymore, and you really have to add other things into the mix. This is for two reasons, the first being you have to get enough people out to buy your apples and pumpkins and peaches and so forth. Also, the second income from playgrounds, hayrides, corn mazes, bonfires, birthday parties and those kinds of outside activities from production and farm things helps to keep the orchard afloat.

We bought the farm here in 2003 and, over the course of the winter, restructured and refurbished it. In that process, we built out the entertainment piece on the farm that has been very successful and grown quite quickly. Each year, we change and grow and do something new to keep people's interest.

What's next?

This year, we put a gem mine in on the farm for the kids; we're the only one around except maybe in Louisville. The year before, we added a five-decker tree house with about five or six slides going out of it. For next year, I'll just have to ponder about that over the winter. We might put in another inflatable, but nothing too big because we don't want to look like everyone else's Saturday flea market park. I haven't come up with any super-duper new mousetrap yet, but I'll be thinking on it.

How many varieties of apples?

I'm going to guess we have about twenty varieties out there right now.

What are some of the best kinds of apples for making applesauce?

Jonathan always was and always will be the old standby, go-to apple for making apple butter. A Golden Delicious also is really excellent both for sauce and for apple butter. We have Jonagolds, which is a combination of those two apples, so it works nicely as well.

What are some good pie-making apples?

We have one in the summer called Early Gold; it sometimes goes by the name of a June Apple, and it's a direct descendant—more than 50 percent of its genetics—from the Lodi. That is an excellent pie apple. It's a little on the tart side; if you like a pie that's a little less sweet, that would be a great choice. We like to blend apples. For our apple cider, we'll blend five different varieties for that and three for apple pies. We like to include a Honey Crisp, a Jonagold, maybe even just a Jonathan to put some tartness in it. Blending is good, even though a Jonathan by itself will make delicious sauce and apple butter. I just think any time you blend you change the sugars and acids a little bit and works better.

What's the most interesting that's ever happened at the orchard?

Something happened Saturday that's a pretty good example of how I get rewarded every day. I was standing around the doorway, and a group of kids was coming out from a hayride. The dad stopped me and said, "Are you Mr. Boyd? I'm just letting you know that we had the best time here today! Everything was perfect, and the kids loved it. We want to come back every year." When you hear things like that, it's a huge reward and makes it all worth it. That's something you really feed off of.

Of course, we have calamities that occur sometimes with our crops. Last year, we froze out about 60 to 75 percent of our trees; it all happened in about a two-hour window in the morning. You have that kind of mental anguish to deal with, just like days that are rainouts. Rainouts are particularly bad for us because it's like we're all dressed up and ready to go to the dance, and Mother Nature comes along and cancels the dance. Those kinds of things you have no control over but hit really hard—those are pretty difficult sometimes.

When you have a business without a roof over it, you're weather subject. If you're silly enough like us to be in a business like that, you need to have enough strength to be able to withstand the bad licks. It's just like if you were a restaurant and all you had was outdoor seating, you have to man up and take the consequences because you know they're coming!

What's your favorite kina oj apple uessert.

I'm a standard apple pie person—just a slice of apple pie for me. We do a fried apple pie here with dried apples; it's really old-fashioned, and the recipe is about one hundred years old. Personally, I detest that thing. I can't eat it. We sell twenty-some-odd-thousand every year, though, and people just keep coming back for them. Everyone doesn't have the same taste buds, and our apple pie to me is as good as I've ever eaten. I'm super satisfied with that. Our signature item here is our apple cider doughnut: we sold a quarter of a million of them last year. It's an extremely popular item.

About how many folks visit each year?

It's a little bit of a guess, but it's an educated guess: the conservative number would be about 75,000 but probably closer to 100,000. We'll have about 4,000 to 5,000 on one Saturday in October.

Part 2

DERBY

◆

FAVORITES

Soundtrack for the Derby Day Party

"The Race Is On" by George Jones
"Wild Horses" by the Rolling Stones
"Paradise" by John Prine
"Blue Moon of Kentucky" by Bill Monroe
"Blue Kentucky Girl" by Loretta Lynn
"Stewball Was a Race Horse" by the Hollies
"Camptown Races" by Johnny Cash
"The Angels Took My Racehorse Away" by Richard Thompson
"Better Off Betting On a Horse" by Betty Grable
"Derby Day" by Jerry Jeff Walker
"Chestnut Mare" by the Byrds
"I Dig a Pony" by the Beatles

INGREDIENT SPOTLIGHT: BAKING WITH BOOZE

Along with fast women and beautiful horses, bourbon is a staple of Kentucky's tipsy heritage and makes a cameo in any number of recipes, both sweet and savory. While at first blush, it might seem like the mixing of alcohol and sugar is simply a way to indulge in multiple forms of gluttonous revelry, there is actually a precise science in order to ensure the proper flavors develop.

adding a richness and depth of flavor in a way that many extracts are unable to provide. One safe bet with which to begin experimenting is replacing rum for vanilla extract in any sort of sugar cookie or pound cake.

Sweating It Out: Not to dispute what your mother told you, but the old adage, "the liquor is cooked out of it!" in reference to dishes created with alcoholic beverages, is probably not the case. Depending on the cook time, between 5 and 85 percent of alcohol content is retained by confections. For a cake that bakes for 1 hour in the oven, 65 percent of the boozy goodness will stay put.

Easy Does It: While it might be tempting to add the maximum amount of liquor called for in the beginning, go slow and add liquor little by little to ensure that the confection doesn't end up tasting like a shot.

TIPS AND TRICKS

Oh Nuts!: While pecans are the traditional nut of a May Day Pie, a combination of walnuts and pecans is able to provide a rich, earthy texture alongside the buttery richness of the pecans. Also, play around with nut combinations from local Kentucky nuts, such as butternuts or hickory nuts.

Selecting Bourbon: The use of a high-quality bourbon in both the pie crust and the filling is key. Knob Creek, bottled just miles away from the Derby's home at the Churchill Downs racetrack, has the ideal oaky, toasted nuttiness to help the savory flavors in the pie shine. For the dark liquor enthusiasts among us, a light coating of bourbon around the inside of the pie crust prior to pouring the filling can pack a subtle, but noticeable, punch once the pie leaves the oven and makes the dish a decidedly adult treat.

Nap Time: Refrigerating the dough is particularly important for the crust in order to properly absorb the bourbon flavoring. While two hours is the minimum amount of time required in a pinch, if the dough is able to cool out in the refrigerator overnight, your pie's crust will be an extra delicious treat.

SIDEKICK COCKTAIL
MINT JULEP

Yield: 1 cocktail

6 springs of mint
1½ teaspoons sugar
3 ounces bourbon

Chill a sterling silver or pewter julep cup in the freezer for 1 hour. Place roughly 6 mint leaves in the bottom of the julep cup, then add sugar and muddle. Pack julep cup ¼ of the way full with crushed ice. Pour bourbon over the ice. Stir briskly until the glass frosts. Add more ice and stir again before serving. Stick a few sprigs of mint into the ice so that the partaker will get the aroma.

SIDEKICK RECIPE
MINT JULEP BROWNIES

Yield: 24 servings
Active Time: 20 minutes * Total Time: 40 minutes
Special Tools: 8x8-inch square pan

5 sprigs fresh mint
¾ cup granulated sugar
4 ounces cream cheese, softened
¼ cup unsalted butter, softened
2 large eggs, room temperature
1½ cups all-purpose flour

½ teaspoon baking powder
¼ teaspoon salt
1 ounce dark (80% cacao) chocolate
1 teaspoon peppermint oil
1 cup confectioners' sugar
3 teaspoons bourbon

In a small bowl, muddle mint leaves with granulated sugar. Allow to stand for a minimum of 4 hours and preferably overnight.

Preheat oven to 350°F and grease pan generously with butter, then dust with flour. Remove mint leaves from sugar. Using a handheld electric mixer, cream together cream cheese, butter and sugar until light and fluffy. Add eggs to mixture one at a time, mixing until completely combined. Sift flour, baking powder and salt into the wet mixture, stirring g

Taking two small medium bowls, melt one chocolate square in the first bowl and fill with half the batter, mixing to combine. Place the remainder of the batter in second bowl, then mix in peppermint oil. Pour chocolate batter in the pan, followed by the mint batter. Drag a butter knife in a zigzag pattern to marbleize the batter. Bake until a toothpick inserted in the center comes out clean, about 20 minutes.

Once cooled, sift confectioners' sugar into a small bowl. Add in bourbon and whisk until smooth. Pour glaze over brownies and allow to cool. Serve immediately.

MAY DAY PIE

Yield: 1 9-inch pie
Active Time: 35 minutes * Total Time: 1 hour, 30 minutes

For the Crust:
- 1¼ cups all-purpose flour
- ¼ teaspoon salt
- 1 teaspoon sugar
- 10 tablespoons unsalted butter, frozen
- 2 tablespoons bourbon, chilled
- 3 tablespoons ice water

For the Filling:
- 2 medium eggs, beaten
- ¾ cup all-purpose flour
- ½ cup white sugar
- ½ cup dark brown sugar
- 1 cup unsalted butter, melted
- ¼ cup dark corn syrup
- ¼ cup bourbon
- 1 cup dark (73 percent cacao) chocolate chips
- ½ cup chopped walnuts
- ½ cup chopped pecans

For the Crust:

Pulse flour, salt and sugar together in food processor. Add butter a tablespoon at a time, pulsing until the mixture forms small, pea-sized clumps. Add bourbon one tablespoon at a time, followed by ice water. Pulse until the dough becomes moist and begins to pull away from the sides. Form the dough into a ¼-inch-thick disc. Secure with plastic wrap and refrigerate a minimum of 2 hours. Press into pie plate.

For the Filling:

Adjust oven rack to center position and preheat oven to 350°F. Whisk together eggs, flour and both sugars in a large bowl. Once combined, add melted butter followed by corn syrup, stirring continuously. Fold in bourbon, chocolate chips and nuts. Pour into prepared pie crust and bake until top is firm and golden, about 55 minutes. Allow to cool slightly and then serve.

SWEET SOUND OFF:
WALTER LUPE
KERN'S KITCHEN

While this might be the favorite pie of the Kentucky Derby, it also has one of the most controversy-rich histories of any dessert out there today. While most know this dish colloquially as Derby Pie®, the name is a registered trademark of local pie company Kern's Kitchen and cannot be used to describe the dessert in any sort of official capacity. The alternative "May Day" namesake springs from the famous horse race's annual time slot—the first Saturday in May—but the regional favorite can also be seen dappling dessert tables and luncheon spreads under the name Pegasus or Horse Race Pie. Walter Lupe traces the fascinating history of the pie and its rich history of litigation.

Could you tell me a little bit about the history of Kern's Kitchen?
My name is Walter Lupe. I'm the grandson of Walter and Leondra Kern, the two people who were critical in starting the Kern's Kitchen business. They were running a restaurant just outside of Louisville called the Melrose Inn in the early to mid-1950s, and they developed our Derby

were pleased with, the name actually came about by putting a bunch of names in a hat one evening after they were finished cooking with several folks sitting around, and Derby Pie® was the one that was pulled out. They just continued to make the pie for the restaurant for the next ten or so years until the mid-1960s, when they gave up running the restaurant and just continued with the pie business. The business serviced some of the nicer restaurants in Louisville at the time, and when I came into the business, they had about thirteen or fourteen restaurant customers they made their pies for.

When did they trademark the name Derby Pie®?
They got the name Derby Pie® registered sometime in the mid-1960s with both the state and the federal government and received the official registration from the United States Patent and Trademark Office in October of 1968.

I know you've been in a few legal battles about the name.

It's really something that when you do a registered trademark, it's your job to police and protect it. It is something that we've given some time to over the years—we've been in about ten major pieces of litigation to protect the name. In the late 1980s, we were in litigation with *Bon Apétit*, and before we even had a day in court, the judge ruled based on filings that the name was generic. We filed for appeal on that and went up to the Sixth Circuit Court of Appeals in Cincinnati. It took a year to run it through, but they reversed the decision.

Are you a crust person or a filling person?

We make our own crust here from scratch, and we're real proud of our crust. It's from Grandma's recipe box, and it's the same recipe that was passed on to me back in the early 1970s. I think the crust is a major part of our pie, especially if you serve it warm; it's a real blend between the chocolate and walnuts, and when you add the crust on the back end of that that's light and flaky, you get the crunch of the nuts, the richness of the chocolate and then the flakiness of the crust. You get a lot of different taste treats going on when you eat the pie.

What are some recent Kern's developments?

We came out with our golden pecan pie in 2009, and it's our first new product in probably forty years. We're kind of unusual in the business in the fact that we're so specialized; we're small batch. The golden pecan pie was a recipe that was in Grandma Kern's recipe box, and we modified it to be able to do it on a larger scale. We use big jumbo pecans, flash them off a little bit so you get a little bit more crunch on the nut. It's kind of an unusual pecan pie because it's not quite as sweet—a lot of pecan pies, in our opinion, are overly sweet. We use our own shell on that also, so it's a very nice piece of pie.

How many Derby Pies® do you produce a year?

We're in the 130,000 to 150,000 range. I know that probably sounds like a pretty big number, but the big pie companies probably turn that out in a day.

What's it like to serve Derby Pie® during Derby?

Derby time is definitely our Mount Everest! We start climbing it at about the end of February every year, and it's a monster season for us. The pie is sold all year round, but Derby is really our challenge—our challenge and our fun time.

Have you ever served any celebrities?
There was a great horn player by the name of Al Hurt who was in town during the Derby one year. He called us up on Derby day, and I think that's probably the only time I've ever delivered a pie on the day of the Derby because generally if we make it to that Saturday, we take the day off. He was a special consideration, and I was such a fan of his, so we got some pies down to him at a local hotel when he called for them.

Few dishes are able to dance along the sweet-savory line quite like spoonbread, which is easily able to pull double duty as a cheesy side dish or smothered in syrup for an after-dinner treat. While spoonbread didn't appear in a cookbook until Sarah Rutledge's *The Carolina Housewife* in 1847, the dish has a rich Native American history. In her original recipe, Ms. Rutledge refers to spoonbread as "Awendaw Spoon Bread," after the Awendaw Indians from in and around Charleston who were known as some of the most prolific corn growers in the region.

In Kentucky, Boone Tavern has long been associated with spoonbread, as the dish is a staple of the dining room's menu and draws people from across the country. The dish is always served steaming hot and smeared in fresh, local butter. In previous eras, a garnish of pickled watermelon rinds would also accompany it when served as an appetizer.

SPOONBREAD VERSUS CORN PUDDING VERSUS CORN SOUFFLÉ

While each dish has corn at its very heart, it's the execution that makes these delicacies uniquely their own.

Spoonbread: With more similarities to corn soufflé than corn bread, spoonbread is a cornmeal or corn flour baked dish that rises like a soufflé but has the earthy, down-home texture of corn bread.

Corn Pudding: Absent of any flour or meal, corn pudding really lets the corn shine through. The dish usually combines the vegetable in a casserole dish with cheese, milk mixture and various spices.

Corn Soufflé: Its light, airy nature is the hallmark of corn soufflé, accomplished through whipping the eggs to incorporate air. Additionally, corn soufflé is traditionally served in individual ramekins and without cornmeal, which allows the dish to form a dignified, bouffant-style puff.

HISTORIC AND SIGNATURE KENTUCKY TAVERNS

Kentucky is home to some of the best-preserved taverns in the United States, rich with tales of famous guests and key in the history of the state's food and beverage heritage. While *inn* and *tavern* once held separate meanings—inns served wine, while taverns served beer and ale—the two terms blended together as colonists made their way from the British Isles to the United States.

Beginning in the mid-1700s, taverns were points of gathering, rest and nourishment for travelers across the Midwest and South traversing the hills and valleys from New England to explore the untamed wilds. Due to the fact that towns themselves were few and far between, taverns became landmarks and essential for not only travelers but also local farmers as gathering places to discuss news, soil conditions and crop prices.

Several Kentucky inns, in addition to Boone Tavern, soon became synonymous with signature dishes, taking up a position as culinary landmarks in the commonwealth's history.

Tallbott Inn: This inn, located in Bardstown, Kentucky, lays claim to the fact that it is America's oldest western stagecoach stop, as well as the world's first bourbon bar. Many of Kentucky's most notorious bourbon families—the Beams, the Samuels and more—were regulars of the tavern and sought the advice and support of tavern owners when beginning their distilleries. Their Kentucky burgoo, a signature stew of the commonwealth typically made with mutton, is a heritage recipe.

Beaumont Inn: Located in Harrodsburg, Kentucky, Beaumont Inn is known for its "yellow-legged" fried chicken, corn pudding, General Robert E. Lee orange-lemon cake and two-year aged Kentucky country ham. While most country ham in the state is aged for one year, the special process used by Beaumont Inn takes extra advantage of the seasonal fluctuations of temperature and humidity in central Kentucky, using a special "aging house" behind the inn.

SIDEKICK COCKTAIL
CORN 'N OIL

Yield: 1 cocktail

2 ounces dark rum
½ ounce sorghum syrup
⅓ ounce fresh lime juice
2–3 dashes Angostura bitters
lime wedge, garnish

Fill a lowball or old-fashioned glass with crushed ice. Add the rest of the ingredients and stir until well chilled. Add the lime garnish and serve.

SPOONBREAD FESTIVAL

The Spoonbread Festival is held every autumn in Berea, Kentucky, a small town in the foothills of Appalachia known as the "Folk Arts and Crafts Capital" of the state and home to the spoonbread mecca Boone Tavern. Since the first festival in 1996, Berea has become synonymous with the dish, hosting a weekend-long event in celebration of its heritage and complete with contradancing, spoonbread-eating contests and plenty of fine bluegrass music.

SIDEKICK RECIPE
CORNMEAL COOKIES WITH APPLE CIDER GLAZE

Yield: 24 cookies
Active Time: 20 minutes * Total Time: 30 minutes

For the Cookies:
1¾ cups all-purpose flour
1 cup yellow cornmeal
1 teaspoon baking soda
¾ teaspoon coarse salt
8 tablespoons unsalted butter
1¼ cups light brown sugar

1 teaspoon pure vanilla extract
2 large eggs

For the Glaze:
1 cup confectioners' sugar
1 tablespoon light corn syrup
2 tablespoons apple cider

Preheat oven to 350°F. Line a baking sheet with parchment paper and set aside. Whisk together flour, cornmeal, baking soda and salt in a large bowl. In a large bowl, using a handheld electric mixer, beat butter and sugar until light, incorporated after each addition. Add dry ingredients to butter mixture ¼ at a time, mixing after each addition. Using a tablespoon, drop 1-inch dough mounds onto prepared tray about 2 inches apart. Bake until lightly browned on the edges, about 10 minutes. Let cool and add glaze.* Serve immediately or store in an airtight container for up to 5 days.

For the Glaze: Sift confectioners' sugar into a medium bowl. Stir in corn syrup and apple cider until completely combined. Use immediately or stir glaze prior to using each time.

SPOONBREAD

Yield: 1 9-inch round pan
Active Time: 30 minutes * Total Time: 1 hour, 50 minutes

3 cups whole milk
1¼ cups cornmeal
3 tablespoons butter, melted
1 teaspoon baking powder
1 teaspoon fine salt
2 large eggs, beaten

Preheat oven to 350°F. Grease pan generously with butter and set aside. In a heavy-bottom saucepan over high heat, bring milk to a boil, whisking consistently. Once the milk begins to boil, add cornmeal in a steady stream while continuing to whisk. Whisk until cornmeal is incorporated into the milk, about 30 seconds.

Remove the pan from the heat and let cool until mixture has reached room temperature. Transfer the mixture to the bowl of a standing mixer fitted with a paddle attachment. Add butter, baking powder, salt and eggs. Mix on medium speed until completely combined and fluffy, about 15 minutes. Pour batter into prepared pan and bake until golden brown and puffy and a toothpick inserted in the center comes out clean, about 1 hour and 20 minutes. Serve immediately with additional butter.

SWEET SOUND OFF:
REID CONNELLY

Reid Connelly, a lifelong Madison County resident and son of longtime Berea mayor Steve Connelly, weighed in on growing up surrounded by spoonbread, as well as just what the dish means to his hometown.

What are some of the key characteristics of a dish like spoonbread that make it reflective of the culture of Berea as a community?

I don't know if Berea and spoonbread share any characteristics, but the origins of spoonbread in Berea definitely share some similarities. Berea has always been a community that is welcoming to others and to celebrating different cultures. Spoonbread was the creation of one of those people who Berea welcomed: Richard Halgon, who was the head chef and director of Boone Tavern. He came to Berea from New England, ran the tavern for many years and was a professor of hotel management at Berea College. This was before I-75 was built and U.S. 25 was the main connection from Michigan to Florida. Boone Tavern was a nice rest stop for travels, and Halgon soon became known for his southern recipes, including spoonbread. This definitely made Berea and Boone Tavern a destination for travelers.

Describe your most memorable spoonbread experience (i.e., family recipes, dinners, Thanksgiving and so on).

Several years ago, I was seeing a girl whose family drove through Berea on a visit. While here, they had spoonbread at Boone Tavern and really loved it! A few weeks later, she mentioned to me that her mother made some spoonbread back at home but it was just not the same. She said that the butter was not right and asked if I could, somehow, get some of the shaped (flower print I think) butter from Boone Tavern. When I told this story to the staff at Boone Tavern, I received some very confused looks, but I came away with some butter.

What are some other pieces of Berea culture that you see as inextricably linked to unique foodways (if any)?

Berea is a community that embraces and helps to promote local artists. This is not limited to jewelers, potters and woodworkers but also to culinary artists. The Kentucky Artisan Center, which is located on the outskirts of Berea, has several selections of Kentucky foods from cookbooks to spices and candies. If you're making a trip through town to taste some of the local dishes, College Square—located conveniently in the town center—can offer some of Berea's favorite restaurants like Boone Tavern (for spoonbread) or Papalenos (for the signature Mountaineer pizza).

Heritage recipes have taken on a newfound popularity in the wake of the recent farm-to-table movement nationally. Do you feel like this emphasis on exporting "authentic" dishes has the potential to harm communities?

I don't think it harms communities. I think the exportation of spoonbread has helped with Berea's popularity. Spoonbread is honestly not one of the first things I think of when describing Berea to others, but many outside of the community have linked it to Berea. So I think that has only benefited our community. If you want to talk about heritage recipes, my mom has one for squash spoonbread that I hear is fantastic. Unfortunately, I don't like squash.

My dad also has a cookbook that was written by a former Berea College student and Berea resident called *More than Moonshine*. The author is Sidney Saylor Farr, and the book was published in 1983, so I guess you could say that Berea has been exporting our recipes for quite some time.

Has the Spoonbread Festival worked to reinforce this dish as a cultural community touchstone? If so, has it been successful at bridging the gap between generations?

I think the festival has evolved over the years to become more than just a time to get spoonbread. I think this is an attempt to involve more generations of citizens in our community and to attract others. The festival features many different vendors, entertainment and even an annual tractor show. Spoonbread just happens to be served and is a great excuse for everyone to have an enjoyable weekend and is a nice complement to the many other festivals that Berea hosts throughout the year.

BOURBON BALLS

*W*hile there will never be a shortage of liquor during a Kentucky Derby celebration, the omission of bourbon balls from a festive spread would be almost as big of a faux pas as leaving the Four Roses at home. The buttercream center is overwhelmingly rich and can be made flecked with bits of pecans or without. The importance of wrapping each center individually while freezing is critical to the candy-making process and will bode well for their success when they are ready to take a chocolate dip.

SPOTLIGHT: DIPPING CHOCOLATE

All sweets enthusiasts have their preference as to which dipping chocolate is superior. While each has its strengths and drawbacks, when choosing a chocolate for bourbon balls, the type selected will heavily influence the outcome of the dish.

Dark Chocolate: In order to best complement the bourbon flavor of the candy, dark chocolate is far and away your best option. A baking chocolate with at least 80 percent cacao brings the richest, deepest flavor.

Milk Chocolate: If you're a milk chocolate devotee, use a chocolate with 40 percent cacao in order to accent the malty, vanilla notes of the bourbon balls.

White Chocolate: Seriously, just don't.

TIPS AND TRICKS

Melon Mechanics: Use a melon baller when forming the interior of the bourbon balls in order to ensure size consistency. If the ball shape doesn't emerge perfectly, always use gloves when reshaping to avoid pulling apart the candy or overheating it.

When I Dip, You Dip: Looking for a simple way to dip your bourbon balls in chocolate without a giant mess? Insert a toothpick into the top, fondue-style, and dip to your heart's content.

I'm Melting: Melting chocolate for coating the bourbon balls presents the very real, unappetizing risk of burning the chocolate. In order to avoid this fate, temper the chocolate by adding ¼ cup more of chopped chocolate pieces when the chocolate is almost melted and stir constantly until the mixture is smooth. This method will activate the sugar crystals in a manner that ensures that the chocolate stays firm at room temperature.

Water, Water Everywhere: Never allow water to come into contact with melting chocolate. A drop or two of water can make the chocolate seize up, becoming a hard, lumpy mess.

Mellow Out: Some argue that bourbon balls should be allowed to mellow—much like bourbon itself—overnight or for a period of days before consumption, but I've always found that to be quite the impossible task.

The Great Debate: There is a great deal of debate across Kentucky about which version of the bourbon ball is the authentic variety: those dipped in chocolate and garnished with a pecan half or those rolled in powdered sugar. While the Ruth Hunt candy company has popularized the chocolate-dipped variety, the earliest cookbooks tend to err on the side of the powdered sugar rolled version. In the late 1800s, the bourbon ball had much more in common with the rum balls seen at holiday parties than a chocolate candy bar. The development of the state's sweet tooth and taste for chocolate, though, has made the chocolate-dipped version far more common on dessert tables across the commonwealth.

Bourbon in Song

"Jockey Full of Bourbon" by Tom Waits
"Bourbon from Heaven" by Dean Martin

SIDEKICK COCKTAIL
BOURBON BALL COCKTAIL

Yield: 1 cocktail

1½ ounces bourbon
½ ounce crème de cacao
½ ounce hazelnut liqueur
1 ounce heavy cream
chocolate shavings, for garnish

Combine first three ingredients, shake with ice and pour into a martini glass. Top with cream and garnish with chocolate shavings.

BOURBON BALLS

Yield: 20 1-inch bourbon balls
Active Time: 30 minutes * Total Time: 3 hours, 30 minutes
Special Tools: parchment paper, plastic wrap

½ cup unsalted butter, melted
3½ cups confectioners' sugar
7 tablespoons top-shelf bourbon
¼ cup crushed pecans
¾ cup semisweet chocolate chips
2 tablespoons whole milk
20–30 pecan halves

Combine butter, sugar and bourbon in a bowl and beat with a wooden spoon or an electric mixer on low speed until smooth. Fold in crushed pecans until evenly distributed. Refrigerate mixture for 1 hour. Using a melon baller, form mixture into 1-inch balls. Place balls on a baking pan lined with parchment paper. Refrigerate until firm. Remove balls, wrap individually with plastic wrap and freeze for a minimum of 2 hours.

Combine chocolate chips and whole milk in double boiler over medium heat, stirring until melted. One at a time, use a dipping fork (or toothpick) to submerge buttercream balls in chocolate, coating on all sides.

Place on baking pan lined with parchment paper and garnish with pecan halves. Allow balls to completely harden before eating.

*I*f the Kentucky Derby already covers several notorious vices as an event (betting on horse races, drinking bourbon, smoking cigars), it's fitting to just round out that list with a glorious, gluttonous cake. The Kentucky butter cake lives up to the hype of its name with a heaping lot of butter in both the batter and glaze while still managing to maintain a refined, well-balanced flavor that will be a winner with all members of the family.

Event Spotlight:

Host a Cakewalk

The Kentucky butter cake is the ideal sweet to bring to everyone's favorite walking-in-circles carnival event, the cakewalk. The cakewalk originated on plantations across the South and Midwest during the 1800s as a kind of dance, which eventually swept the nation and even inspired a genre of ragtime-style music. Fortunately for the less sure-footed among us, cakewalks of today are simply musical chairs with a sweet cake prize. Here's how to host a cakewalk at your next shindig:

Pre-Step One: Have partygoers bring cakes for the cakewalk stash or bake a stockpile of cakes in preparation for the party.

Step One: Lay out numbered squares, 1 through 20, in a circle. (Bonus if the numbered squares are shaped like cakes!)

Step Two: Each partygoer should draw a ticket, with the number of tickets equal to the number of squares in the circle.

Step Three: Partygoers stand on their initial square, music begins to play and partygoers begin to walk around the circle. (Bonus if you play music by the band Cake!)

Step Four: The music stops after a few minutes, the partygoers stop on squares and a number is drawn.

Step Five: The partygoer standing on the corresponding square wins a cake of their choice as a prize.

TIPS AND TRICKS

Glazed Over: The glaze is the crowning jewel of the cake, creating a texture that walks the line between pound cake and a giant Krispy Kreme doughnut. When preparing the glaze, keep a constant, low-to-medium temperature and whisk continuously to ensure that the proper thickness is reached without boiling. If the mixture boils, it will begin to enter into brown butter territory, which completely shifts the nature of the cake.

Early Bird: While the cake is good at any hour of the day, there is something magical about eating it in the most traditional way: early morning and slightly warm.

KENTUCKY BUTTER CAKE

Yield: 1 10-inch Bundt cake
Active Time: 20 minutes * Total Time: 1 hour, 30 minutes
Special Tools: Bundt cake pan

For the Cake:

3 cups all-purpose flour
2 cups light brown sugar
1½ teaspoons baking powder
1 teaspoon baking soda
1 cup half-and-half
1 cup unsalted butter, melted
4 large eggs, room temperature

For the Glaze:

½ cup unsalted butter
1 cup granulated sugar
2 tablespoons vanilla extract

For the Cake:

Preheat oven to 325°F. Grease a 10-inch Bundt pan. Combine flour, sugar, baking powder and baking soda in a medium bowl. Whisk until homogenous. Add half-and-half, butter and eggs. Beat using a handheld electric mixer until combined and pour batter into pan. Transfer to oven and bake until a toothpick inserted in the center comes out clean, about 1 hour.

For the Glaze:

Combine butter, sugar and vanilla in a small saucepan over medium heat. Stir continuously until completely melted and combined. (Do not allow glaze to boil.)

While the cake is still warm and in the pan, use a wooden skewer to poke 8–10 small holes in the cake bottom (the exposed top side). Pour warm glaze slowly over cake. Allow to cool completely, remove from pan and serve.

Part 3

There are few cakes that can please an entire table full of people. Some folks turn up their nose at chocolate, and others wouldn't touch a fruity dessert with a ten-foot pole. Behold, the answer to your picky cake eater problems: the jam cake. This cake, which is largely associated with the holiday season, is the perfect blend of sweet and spice, with a tender crumb soft enough to melt the hearts of even the biggest dessert curmudgeon. It's the Tiny Tim of cakes.

SWEET SPOTLIGHT: CHRISTMAS DESSERTS

No matter what part of the state you visit, Christmas is a time almost directly associated with the delivery of sweets to friends and family. The tradition is akin to a much more festive version of Sunday visiting after church, in which cakes and pies are brought to neighbors for an afternoon of laughing, kids playing and perhaps a little gossiping. Church bake sales, auxiliary dinners and community groups also get in on the mix during the Christmas season, and you'd be hard-pressed to find any sort of holiday event without a table full of sweets for sale accompanying it. Christmas is the most wonderful time of year for home bakers and candy makers to show off the best of their craft—and receive plenty of *oohs* and *ahhs* for their efforts.

> **Literary Note**
> Jam cake is a critical plot point in the novel *Ahab's Wife* by Sena Jeter Naslund.

Black Walnut Fudge

Yield: 18 pieces
Active Time: 20 minutes * Total Time: 5 hours, 20 minutes

2 cups sorghum syrup
1 tablespoon corn syrup
½ cup heavy cream
¼ cup whole milk

½ cup black walnuts, coarsely chopped
1½ teaspoons vanilla extract

Grease a baking dish generously with butter, then set aside. Combine sorghum, corn syrup, cream and milk in a heavy-bottom saucepan, attach a candy thermometer and cook over medium heat. Cook, without stirring, until the mixture reaches soft ball stage, around 238°F.

Remove the pan from the heat and let cool until mixture is still warm but cool enough to touch. Using a handheld electric mixer, beat the mixture until it begins to thicken, lose its shine and become lighter, about 8 minutes. Working quickly, add in walnuts and vanilla until evenly distributed. Pour fudge into a greased baking dish and set aside to harden for a minimum of 5 hours. Cut fudge into bite-sized pieces and store in a tin. The fudge can be kept up to two weeks.

Rum Balls

Yield: 20–30 rum balls
Active Time: 15 minutes * Total Time: 2 hours, 15 minutes

1 cup vanilla wafers, ground
1 cup pecans, finely chopped
1 cup confectioners' sugar
1 teaspoon cinnamon

½ teaspoon nutmeg
¼ cup cocoa powder
¼ cup rum
2 tablespoons corn syrup

Using a food processor, pulse vanilla wafers until they are the texture of a coarse meal. In a medium bowl, whisk together ground wafers, pecans, confectioners' sugar, spices and cocoa powder until well combined. Add rum and corn syrup until all ingredients combine and begin to pull together. Using a melon baller, form into ½-inch balls and roll in confectioners' sugar. Chill for a minimum of 2 hours and serve immediately. The balls can be kept in a cool, dry place for up to a week.

TIPS AND TRICKS

Jam Out: While it might not make a difference for your morning toast, it's incredibly important to use jam—not jelly—in the jam cake. The consistency and texture of jam is what helps make the jam cake moist and buoyant.

To Frost or Not to Frost: There are some jam cake purists who believe that the cake is best served naked—no frosting allowed. This method makes the cake a more informal, everyday confection, coated with just a light dusting of powdered sugar. The frosting, though, is what many people enjoy the most about the cake, making it a decadent treat for holidays and parties.

Caramel Catastrophe: For those not indoctrinated into the world of boiled icing, making caramel frosting can seem like a bit of a headache. It runs the gamut from one extreme (thick as a brick and impossible to cut) to the other (runny and like a lackluster glaze). The most important trick to avoiding extremist frosting is to stir constantly and apply immediately to the cooled cake when it reaches the "soft ball" stage (approximately 238°F and you can spread it around). If it cooks any longer and begins to harden, add in 2–3 tablespoons of heavy cream to loosen it back up.

JAM CAKE

Yield: 1 3-tier 9-inch cake
Active Time: 30 minutes * Total Time: 2 hours
Special Tools: 3 9-inch cake pans

For the Cake:

5 large eggs, room
    temperature
½ cup golden raisins
¼ cup pecans
¼ cup walnuts
3 cups all-purpose
    flour
1 cup unsalted butter
2 cups light brown
    sugar

1 teaspoon baking soda
1 cup buttermilk
½ teaspoon salt
1 teaspoon cloves
1 teaspoon cinnamon
1 teaspoon allspice
1 teaspoon nutmeg
2 teaspoons vanilla
    extract
1 cup blackberry jam
2 teaspoons bourbon

For the Frosting:

½ cup unsalted butter
1 cup light brown sugar
¼ cup heavy cream
1 teaspoon bourbon
3 cups confectioners'
    sugar

For the Cake:

Preheat oven to 350°F, grease baking pans generously with butter and dust with flour. Separate eggs and beat whites with a handheld electric mixer until soft peaks are formed. Set aside. In a small bowl, dredge raisins and nuts in flour and set aside.

In a medium bowl, cream butter with a handheld electric mixer on medium speed, adding sugar in a steady stream until combined. Add egg yolks one at a time, beating well after each addition. Alternating baking soda first, then buttermilk, add both to butter mixture, stirring after each addition. Fold in spices, vanilla and bourbon. Add jam to batter, beating on low speed until completely combined. Gently fold in egg whites. Bake until a toothpick inserted in the center of each cake comes out clean, about 35 minutes.

For the Frosting:

In a heavy-bottom saucepan over medium heat, melt butter and add brown sugar, whisking until combined. Bring mixture to a boil and cook 1 minute, continuing to whisk; add cream and bourbon and stir until combined. In a steady stream, begin slowly adding confectioners' sugar until frosting is totally combined. Once cake has cooled, frost immediately. The cake can be kept in an airtight container for up to 5 days.

Sweet Sound Off:
David Baird

When culinary history is discussed in the commonwealth, the influence of the baby boomer era is largely overlooked, with the majority of attention paid solely to older (pre–World War II) recipes and their current resurgence. David Baird—a lifelong Kentucky resident and my father—shares some sweet thoughts about growing up in a time of growth and progress.

What kind of desserts were your favorite growing up?
I grew up in a time when a lot of the smaller bakeries around where I grew up were shutting down; we had a great bakery that just couldn't compete with all the new fast-food places coming in offering ice creams and so forth. Also, it was an era where instant mixes were popular and new, so people were really excited about those. JIF made a fudge mix that didn't require adding anything more than water to get it to set up. I would make that every day when I came home from school, let it dry and eat it before my mom got home from work. They made a chocolate and a caramel, but the caramel was my favorite, which probably explains why I like the jam cake icing so much.

I cooked a lot for myself after school, but I didn't do a whole ton of baking when I was really young. I also really liked candies a lot—circus peanuts were maybe my favorite candy then.

When did you have your first jam cake?
It was around 1966. I was fourteen years old, and a woman who worked with my mom at the courthouse in Madison County, the county clerk, made it for us. It's that caramel icing that I really remember: it's just like a Sugar Daddy melted down on top of a cake. I know some folks just make their jam cakes dusted with powdered sugar, but without that icing, for me it's just not the same. Jam cake is a Christmas dessert primarily, and after that year, she would give us a jam cake each December.

What other kinds of sweets did you eat around the holidays?
We would make gingerbread loaves—not gingerbread men. We did a few candies, mainly ribbon candy, but generally nothing too heavy on the chocolate side of things because it was really expensive.

What kind of jam or jelly is best for jam cake?
Blackberry, of course.

What were some sweets at local places?
I really loved to eat the cherry pie that they had at Jerry's J-Boy restaurant, a regional chain across the state of Kentucky that closed in the 1980s. We had a small drive-in, too, that served a classic soft-serve. They would dip the ice cream in a flavoring upside-down that would harden in a shell around the ice cream. They had a chocolate flavor and a cherry flavor, but the cherry was by far my favorite. It sounds standard now, but at the time, it was really exciting to see that an ice cream cone could be made red!

In the baby boomer era, how did sweets change?
The economy just became much more mobile very quickly, and while I don't think heritage recipes and family favorites were totally abandoned, as a baby boomer growing up, it was definitely a time when folks in general were more interested in speed and ease than sticking to those old-timey favorites. Especially growing up in a rural area, it was exciting to have all these options for new and "exotic" sweets to eat that didn't require all day to stand in a kitchen and bake. I also think for the first time, both spouses were working, and that hadn't really happened before, which changed

the amount of time devoted to baking in a lot of households.

Talk about your experience winning the Betty Crocker scholarship.

I won a pretty big scholarship from Betty Crocker when I was a senior in high school to go and study food science and nutrition if I wanted to go that route. The competition was based, first, on cooking and, secondly, on a test about general food and cooking knowledge: weights, measurements, best practices and so forth. I scored the best on the test, won the cooking part and beat out all the competition. It was really a source of amusement for everyone because it was the first year that boys were allowed to be a part of the competition, and I won. We were the first group of boys to take home economics courses at the high school. I didn't take the scholarship, but I did keep the other prize: a tiny, 100 percent sterling silver stove charm meant for a charm bracelet that I have to this day.

Were there any fad sweets that you ate growing up that aren't around really anymore?
In the early 1970s, ice milk came along as a substitute for ice cream, and I ate quite a bit of it. It was marketed as a product that was supposed to be a little healthier for folks, but it was a little lacking in body for my taste. It was a fad that I think has totally gone away. Thank goodness, because it wasn't very good at all.

Chocolate Gravy

Chocolate gravy sounds something like a Willy Wonka fantasy (insert Oompa Loompas here), but in reality it's a rural Kentucky favorite that's been a breakfast staple since the Great Depression. During the Depression, meat rations were particularly difficult to come by, making the traditional means of making gravy far more difficult for home cooks. Cocoa powder, however, was sent out regularly as part of relief efforts, leading to the creation of a chocolate substitute during trying times.

Chocolate Gravy Alias
soppin' chocolate

Pro Tip: Tear up three to four biscuits and line the bottom of a bowl with them, then pour chocolate gravy on top. This traditional preparation method allows for as much biscuit to come in contact with as much gravy as possible.

Spotlight:
Depression-Era Dining in Kentucky

While Kentuckians were devastated by the arrival of the Great Depression in ways similar to the remainder of the country, the state's severe economic decline began long before the stock market crash of 1929. The ratification of the Eighteenth Amendment in 1919 hit two of Kentucky's biggest exports—bourbon and beer—particularly hard, causing job loss statewide. In the early part of the twentieth century, there were nearly two hundred Kentucky distilleries and breweries employing more than four thousand people. By the beginning of the Depression, only a smattering of these businesses remained.

Over the course of the Great Depression, President Franklin Roosevelt's New Deal distributed more than $35 million worth of surplus food and money to Kentucky through a program known as the Federal Surplus Relief Corporation (FSRC). Canned meat, grains, cheese and beans were distributed to families across the state affected by the financial struggles of the time. While constant hunger was a problem for Kentuckians, true starvation was rare in more centrally located areas of the state, such and Lexington and Louisville. However, in the mountains of eastern Kentucky, families whose hardship was compounded by the closure of coal mines at an alarmingly rapid rate prior to the Depression often struggled to feed themselves.

In rural areas, foraging and hunting became popular once again as children could be sent to pick nuts and berries, while older relatives hunted for small game such as rabbit, grouse, squirrel and frogs. (Seriously, don't knock frog gigging until you've tried it.)

The sense of self-sufficiency and community that is the backbone of Kentucky belief was only heightened during the Great Depression, as church potlucks and community picnics became ways to share dishes with one another and those less fortunate.

In Kentucky towns along the Ohio River, the Great Flood of 1937 made the hardships of the Great Depression even more devastating. Waves engulfed cities along the banks of the river, cresting at fifty-seven feet and sixty feet, respectively, in Louisville and Paducah. One of the most iconic photos of the 1930s was taken in Louisville shortly after the floodwaters receded and features African American families standing in a long breadline—ironically in front of a billboard proclaiming, "World's Highest Standard of Living."

TIPS AND TRICKS

She's Lump: Uh oh, did you somehow forget to whisk properly and now your chocolate gravy is lumpy? Never fear. Lumpy chocolate gravy is easily fixed by passing the gravy through a sieve or strainer or pureeing it with an immersion blender.

Coffee Talk: Another favorite biscuit topping in eastern Kentucky is coffee— no dunking required. Coffee was frequently mixed with sugar, at about a ¾ to ¼ ratio, and poured over broken-up biscuits. This messy, soppy breakfast treat is still eaten today and known as "soakins."

SIDEKICK COCKTAIL
KENTUCKY COFFEE

Yield: 1 cocktail

1½ ounces top-shelf bourbon
1 ounce cream liqueur
hot, fresh coffee, to fill
whipped cream, garnish

Pour bourbon and cream liqueur into an Irish coffee glass. Stir. Fill the glass with hot coffee. Top off with a dollop of whipped cream.

SIDEKICK RECIPE
KENTUCKY TEA BISCUITS

While cathead biscuits—those light, fluffy delicacies typically associated with southern cooking and delicious breakfasts—are a part of Kentucky's culinary heritage, the Kentucky tea biscuit is far more prevalent. The firm, chewy texture of the biscuit makes it the perfect complement to salty country ham (its typical tea party partner-in-crime) and the rich, luxurious taste of chocolate gravy.

Yield: 15–20 biscuits
Active Time: 20 minutes * Total Time: 45 minutes

2 cups all-purpose flour
4 teaspoons baking powder
½ teaspoon salt
5 tablespoons unsalted butter, cold
⅔ cup heavy cream

Preheat oven to 400°F and grease baking sheet lightly with butter. Combine flour, baking powder and salt together in a medium bowl. Using a pastry cutter, cut in the butter until the dough is coarse and crumbly. Add heavy cream slowly, mixing with a large spoon (or your hands) until dough comes together. Place the dough on a lightly floured surface, knead 3–4 times with the heel of your hand and roll out until 1 inch thick. Using a biscuit cutter or the rim of a drinking glass, cut out biscuits from dough. Bake until biscuits are golden brown, about 25 minutes.

CHOCOLATE GRAVY

Yield: 1½ cups
Active Time: 15 minutes * Total Time: 15 minutes

1 cup granulated sugar
3½ tablespoons cocoa powder
3 tablespoons self-rising flour
1½ cups whole milk
2 tablespoons unsalted butter

Sift sugar, cocoa powder and flour in a medium bowl. Add the milk slowly and stir until completely combined. In a medium heavy-bottom saucepan, melt butter over medium heat. Add cocoa mixture and continue to cook, whisking constantly until the mixture is thick enough to coat the back of a spoon. Serve immediately or keep in an airtight container in the refrigerator for up to 1 week.

The pudding culture of Kentucky is alive and well, as numerous members of this sweet-and-sticky family have made the rounds on kitchen tables and menus across the state for centuries. While until the early twentieth century savory puddings were also regularly served as a side dish accompaniment for meat, puddings primarily have been reserved for an after-dinner treat with city dwellers and rural families alike. The types of pudding popular across the state fall into primarily three categories.

Soaked Bread: Move over, New Orleans—bread pudding has been a staple of Kentucky cuisine dating back to the early 1800s, when day-old bread was able to be reused by baking it into a dessert. A luxurious bourbon sauce is the key to bread pudding's delicious success, as well as the patience to allow the bread to marry with its sweeter elements. Another variation on this theme, called Cabinet Pudding, is a recipe that calls for home cooks to empty out practically their entire cabinet into a pudding with a stale, white bread base.

Creamy Base: One of the first recipes recorded for banana pudding appeared in Mary Harris Frazier's *The Kentucky Receipt Book* in 1903, and it is a shining example of the prevalence of custardy, creamy puddings in Kentucky since before the turn of the century. Queen pudding, rice pudding, custard pudding and suet pudding were all popular Victorian holiday fare.

Woodford Pudding Aliases
Kentucky pudding,
thoroughbred pudding

Fruity: While nonnative fruits were largely hard to come by for Kentuckians, cooking these fruits into a pudding was a way to both enhance their flavors and ensure that they were preserved at least slightly longer than in their raw form. Popular fruit puddings include apple pudding, plum pudding, orange pudding and pineapple pudding.

INGREDIENT SPOTLIGHT: BUTTERMILK

Buttermilk is a staple ingredient for Kentucky dishes, highly prized for centuries because of its ability to store for longer periods of time than sweet whole milk. Until the twentieth century, buttermilk was the liquid left over from churning butter before cream could be skimmed from the whole milk. During the time between when churning ended and when the milk could be skimmed, lactic acid–producing bacteria fermented the milk. The majority of modern buttermilk today is made by adding a lactic acid bacteria culture to pasteurized whole milk, creating the tartness we've all come to expect.

Drink Up: While few would consider buttermilk their beverage of choice, a traditional Appalachian drink called "Blushing Buttermilk" is still popular in southeastern Kentucky today. The drink, which combines 1 cup of buttermilk with ½ cup of tomato juice and 1 teaspoon of lemon, is said to ease upset stomachs and cure toothaches.

Buttermilk 911: A notorious hangover cure in Appalachia combines ½ cup buttermilk with ½ cup Coca-Cola, shaken until combined and fizzy.

Clabber: Another underappreciated member of Appalachia's dairy heritage is clabber, a curdled milk used for leavening before the invention of baking powder. Fresh, raw milk was left out at room temperature, causing the milk to thicken and sour while also keeping it from actually spoiling. Clabber was deceptively simple to make and integral to baking everyday cakes, breads and biscuits. It was brought to Appalachia by way of Scotch settlers, and to this day, it is still frequently referred to as "bonny clabber" or "autumn milk" within the region. The milk even had its own special spoon, with a ninety-degree-angle handle designed for ladling properly.

While pasteurization has largely erased clabber from the everyday diets of Appalachians, it can still be found occasionally as a breakfast item sprinkled with cinnamon and sugar or dotted with raisins.

Make Your Own: If you find yourself shorthanded and need buttermilk for a recipe, it's easy to whip up just the right amount or find a comparable alternative.

Lemon Method: In a 1-cup measuring cup, combine 1 tablespoon of lemon juice with 1 cup of whole milk. Stir and let sit for 5 minutes. When milk is slightly curdled, it's ready to use.

Vinegar Method: In a 1-cup measuring cup, combine ½ tablespoon of white vinegar with 1 cup of whole milk. Stir and let sit for 5 minutes but no longer than 10. When milk is slightly curdled, it's ready to use.

Yogurt Substitute: In a 1-cup measuring cup, mix ¾ cup plain yogurt with ¼ cup water. Use as you would buttermilk.

Cream of Tartar Substitute: In a 1-cup measuring cup, mix ¾ cup whole milk with 1¾ teaspoons cream of tartar. Stir and let sit for 5 minutes but no longer than 10. When milk is slightly curdled, it's ready to use.

Bevy of Buttermilk: Let's face it: the majority of the time, buying buttermilk is for a lone recipe, and the rest of the giant gallon is left to turn ripe in the fridge. Never let good dairy go to waste with these quick, easy recipes that are sure to use up the remainder of everyone's favorite sour milk.

Buttermilk Cinnamon Swirl Bread

Yield: 1 9-inch loaf
Active Time: 20 minutes * Total Time: 1 hour, 10 minutes

2 cups flour
1½ cups sugar, divided
1 teaspoon baking soda
½ teaspoon salt
1¼ cups buttermilk

1 medium egg
1½ teaspoons vanilla extract
¼ cup vegetable oil
1 tablespoon cinnamon

Preheat oven to 350°F. Lightly grease a loaf pan with butter and dust with flour, tapping out the excess. Combine the flour, 1 cup of the sugar, baking soda, salt, buttermilk, egg, vanilla and oil, stirring. In a small bowl, combine cinnamon and the remaining sugar. Pour half of the batter into bread pan; sprinkle with half of the cinnamon-sugar. Spread with remaining batter and sprinkle with remaining cinnamon-sugar; cut through batter with a knife to swirl. Bake until a toothpick inserted near the center comes out clean, about 50 minutes.

Buttermilk Pecan Candy

Yield: 30–40 candies
Active Time: 15 minutes * Total Time: 1 hour, 15 minutes

2 cups granulated sugar
1 teaspoon baking soda
1 cup buttermilk

2 tablespoons unsalted butter
2½ cups pecans, chopped

Combine sugar, baking soda and buttermilk in a heavy-bottom saucepan. Stirring constantly, cook on high heat for 5 minutes. Add butter and pecans, stirring constantly until it reaches soft ball stage. Remove from heat, cool for 2 minutes and then whip until creamy using a wire whisk. Using a tablespoon, drop onto baking sheet lined with parchment paper. Allow to set for at least 1 hour; store in a cool, dry place.

WOODFORD PUDDING

Yield: 1 9x13-inch baking dish (8–10 servings)
Active Time: 30 minutes * Total Time: 1 hour, 20 minutes

For the Cake:
1 stick butter or margarine, softened
1 cup sugar
3 eggs
1 cup blackberry jam
1 cup all-purpose flour
1 teaspoon cinnamon
1 teaspoon allspice
½ cup buttermilk
1 teaspoon baking soda

For the Sauce:
1½ cups brown sugar
¼ cup all-purpose flour
1 cup water, boiling
¼ teaspoon salt
½ stick unsalted butter
2 tablespoons evaporated milk
1 teaspoon vanilla extract

For the Cake:

Preheat oven to 325°F. Grease a 9x13-inch baking dish with butter, dust with flour and set aside. Using an electric handheld mixer, cream butter and sugar until light and fluffy. Add eggs, one at a time, beating until smooth after each egg. Fold in blackberry jam, beating on slow speed until combined. Sift flour, cinnamon and allspice into the wet mixture and beat on medium speed until completely integrated. Pour in buttermilk and add baking soda, mixing until the batter is thick and free of lumps or streaks. Bake until a toothpick inserted in the center comes out clean, about 50 minutes.

For the Sauce:

Combine sugar and flour in a heavy-bottom saucepan over medium heat, and then add boiling water and salt. Using a whisk, mix until ingredients are completely combined. Bring sauce to a boil and cook until the mixture could coat the back of a spoon, about 5 or 6 minutes. Once the desired thickness is reached, remove the mixture from the heat and add butter, milk and vanilla and stir until combined. Serve pudding warm with a generous helping of butterscotch sauce on top. The cake can be kept up to five days covered in an airtight container. The sauce can be stored for up to one month and is a delicious treat over ice cream.

Modjeskas

*I*f there's one romantic gesture that's sure to woo, it's naming a candy after the object of your affection. That's exactly what Louisville candy maker (and French immigrant) Anton Busath did to spotlight just how enamored he had become of Polish actress Helena Modjeska. In the late 1880s, the Shakespearean actress had a large cult following in the United States and often performed in downtown Louisville, where Mr. Busath would watch, dreamy-eyed, during her shows. Ms. Modjeska was also the first person to produce a Henrik Ibsen play in the United States, which she did (*A Doll's House*, of course) in Louisville in 1883.

While the story didn't end quite happily ever after for Mr. Busath and Ms. Modjeska, this caramel-covered marshmallow candy has gone down in history as perhaps the only confection named after an actress.

INGREDIENT SPOTLIGHT: MARSHMALLOWS

The giant marshmallow man in *Ghostbusters*. Sugary "marshmallow"-filled cereals. The chick-shaped Easter treats known as Peeps. For better or worse, everyone's favorite hot chocolate accoutrement has become a symbol of high-processed junk food over the years.

The truth, though, is that marshmallow is actually—wait for it—a plant (*Althaea officinalis*) and was first fashioned into a confection intended for medicinal use. The leaves, stalk and roots of the plant were used by both the Greeks and Egyptians to soothe upset stomachs and sore throats, fashioned into a thick syrup or mixed with honey, figs and nuts. (A spoonful of sugar really does help the medicine go down; oh, Mary Poppins, will you ever not be right?)

It wasn't until the mid-1800s that the marshmallows we know and love began to take their puffy shape. Confectioners in France began to create the grandfather sweet to the marshmallow by whipping together the sticky, gooey sap extracted from the marshmallow plant with sugar and eggs until fluffed up. The process was incredibly time consuming for very little product, though, and gelatin soon replaced actual marshmallow sap in the creations, allowing for faster production and a lighter candy.

The sweet treat gained immense popularity both in Europe and the United States, and by the 1940s, a crafty American manufacturer had devised a way to industrialize the marshmallow-making business, popping out thousands of marshmallows per day for sticky-fingered children everywhere.

In a pinch, you can try to make Modjeskas with those store-bought pillows of fluff they pass off as marshmallows, but there's nothing quite like homemade. Here's how to make it happen.

TIPS AND TRICKS

Slippery When Wet: Your marshmallows might have a wet layer on the bottom after the drying period. If so, blot off the moisture and flip them upside down, with the wet side facing out, to dry again.

Whip It: Do not under-whip your marshmallow batter before pouring it in the pan. It will potentially lead to a soggy, chewy result.

Rain, Rain Go Away: Making Modjeskas on a day that calls for rain is just asking for disaster. Wait until a dry—hopefully cool—day to whip up the confection.

HOMEMADE MARSHMALLOWS

Yield: 25–30 marshmallows
Active Time: 30 minutes * Total Time: 6 hours, 30 minutes
Special Tools: handheld electric mixer, 8x12-inch glass baking dish

2½ tablespoons unflavored gelatin
½ cup cold water
1½ cups granulated sugar
1 cup light corn syrup
¼ teaspoon salt
½ cup water
2 tablespoons pure vanilla extract

Dust a glass baking dish generously with confectioners' sugar and set aside. Place gelatin and ½ cup cold water in a medium-sized bowl and stir, letting stand for 1 hour. In a small saucepan over low heat, clip on your candy thermometer and combine granulated sugar, corn syrup, salt and ½ cup of water, stirring consistently until sugar has completely dissolved. Once syrup is smooth, raise the heat to high, cooking it down without stirring until it reaches hard ball stage, or 244°F on your candy thermometer. Once hard ball stage is reached, remove pan from heat and pour syrup into the softened gelatin, beating on a low speed with a handheld electric mixer. After 1–2 minutes, increase mixer speed to high and add vanilla, beating consistently until mixture is thick, white, fluffy and doubled in size, about 15 minutes. Pour marshmallow mixture into pan while still warm and let stand for a minimum of 6 hours but preferably overnight. When dry, turn marshmallow out of pan and cut into 1-inch pieces. Marshmallows can be made up to four days in advance and stored in an airtight container.

MODJESKAS

Yield: 20–25 candies
Active Time: 30 minutes * Total Time: 40 minutes
Special Tools: candy thermometer

- 2 cups granulated sugar
- 2 cups heavy cream
- 2 tablespoons unsalted butter
- 1¼ cups corn syrup
- ½ teaspoon salt
- 1 tablespoon vanilla extract
- ¾ pound marshmallows*

In a heavy-bottom saucepan, attach a candy thermometer and combine sugar, 1 cup of the cream, butter, syrup and salt and bring to a boil, stirring constantly. Put remaining 1 cup cream in a small pan and heat separately. Once boiling, cover butter mixture briefly with a lid to dissolve remaining sugar crystals on the sides.

When it begins a rolling boil, carefully pour the hot cream into the butter mixture, whisking consistently. Reduce to medium heat and cook, stirring frequently to prevent burning, until the candy thermometer reaches "soft ball" stage, about 238°F. Remove from heat and, working quickly, stir in vanilla.

Once removed from heat, allow caramel to stand for 6–7 minutes before beginning to dip the marshmallows. If marshmallows are dipped too soon, the hot caramel will dissolve them. Drop 2-inch marshmallow square into caramel and then, with a fork, turn it over to coat completely and lift out, pulling the fork over edge of pan so surplus runs back into pan.

Place each piece on a well-greased baking sheet. Allow to set and harden for about 2 hours. When set, wrap each piece separately in wax paper and store in a cool, dry place.

*see "Ingredient Spotlight" section

SWEET SOUND OFF:
ROSE ANN STACY
MUTH'S CANDY SHOP

A stalwart of the Market Street neighborhood in Louisville, Kentucky, for more than half a century, Muth's Candy Shop is home to the original Modjeska recipe. Rose Ann Stacy, co-owner and niece of the original Muth's founders, offers her tips and tricks for Modjeska making and reflects on growing up as a kid in a candy store.

How was Muth's founded?

My great-aunt and -uncle started Muth's, and I've been here off and on since the summer between my seventh- and eighth-grade years. I've not been here constantly—you get married, you have kids, health issues, things like that—but I've been here off and on my whole life.

Uncle Rudy started the business after World War I in 1921 with my Aunt Belle. She continued to work at another wholesale manufacturer, but she would come every night and help him with whatever needed to be done. She took care of the books, things like that, but they were a team—a true team. When Uncle Rudy was in the war, he was a cook, and he said that when he came back from fighting, he was going to have his own candy business and that it was going to be the best. He made that dream come true.

What kind of sweets did you like to eat growing up?

We've been in two locations—the one we're in now and one block west. It sat right where the I-65 overpass is now for Market Street. I like to say we "moved for progress" in 1962 when we came up here. There was a two-story building at the old location, and the dipping room where they dipped all the chocolates was located upstairs. When I was young, being allowed to go upstairs to the dipping room was really special. I'm short now, but I was really short when I was young, very tiny. They used to all say, "You're a tiny little thing!" (I wish they still said that.) They would sit me up on the edge of the dipping table, and I'd get to dip peppermint straws—that's a hard peppermint filled with cream—into the hot dark chocolate. My biggest childhood memory is that when you walked in the door, you would smell peppermint. It was delightful.

What did you think the first time you ate a Modjeska?
I was probably a teenager, I guess, before I ate a Modjeska. I really liked them immediately. It almost melts in your mouth.

There's quite a bit of folklore around the candy. Could you tell us a little bit about it?
As the story goes, all the candy makers in Louisville were friends. When Mr. Busath's candy store on Fourth Street caught fire—which back then that was the place to be in the 1940s. When it caught fire, the portrait of Helena Modjeska that hung in his candy store, which the Modjeska is named for, was one of the only things to survive the fire. I'm sure it needed restoration, but now it hangs in the Filson Club downtown, which is a historical museum.

After the fire, he came and asked Uncle Rudy if he could make the candy in our shop after Uncle Rudy finished for the day. Uncle Rudy said sure because he already had holiday orders and family orders and plenty to be doing. Time passed, and Mr. Busath couldn't find a place to reopen his candy shop on Fourth Street. Eventually, he made the statement, "If I can't be on Fourth Street, I don't want to be anywhere." So, he didn't reopen his business, and as a thank-you, he gave Uncle Rudy the original Modjeska recipe. That's the recipe we use. We don't know if anyone else has it, we just know that we do. We make it the same way today as we did at the very beginning.

How does the caramel get so soft?
It's made with pure butter and a very high-quality grade of cream—no corners are cut.

What advice would you offer the home cook trying to make a Modjeska?
[Laughs] Don't! Not to sound sarcastic, but good luck. There are caramel recipes, but the hardest thing is that the marshmallows sold in the stores are far too soft. They would dissolve in caramel that's been heated thin enough for you to dip it in. There are recipes for homemade marshmallows, and I believe people who say they make their own have made their own marshmallows as well. You don't get that very often, though. You get a lot more people saying that they make their own bourbon balls. I collect cookbooks and have seen in one of my aunt's old cookbooks that covers everything from A–Z a recipe for marshmallows that may work but probably not so. It's different than ours. It's not the original.

What's the hardest part about making Modjeskas?

The weather is the hardest part about making Modjeskas. The more humid it is, the harder we have to get them. Once they get cool enough that we can wrap, we have to get them done right away because they get sticky, and humidity plays a big part in that. It's just like when you're making brittle—humidity plays a big part in that as well.

What's the most fun or interesting thing that's happened in the Muth's store?

Every day is interesting because nothing's the same—that's why I like getting up and coming to work. Every day there are different orders; there are different customers. I really like it.

We've had tons of celebrities come in during Derby time, but my favorite are the local personalities, including lots of big corporation heads and television anchors. They help spread the word. She doesn't work for television anymore, but Jackie Hays [a local Louisville newscaster], her mother's favorite candy was the Modjeska. Even being a newscaster, a personality, she'd wait in line for the Modjeskas like everyone else. She is the sweetest thing. Everyone we deal with we really love. We wouldn't be here this long without our customers. We really feel like that's the best part of being in the business is making them happy. They'll worry sometimes and say, "Oh, I'm sorry I took up so much of your time!" but that's what we're here for, to please them.

Some of our most popular things, not necessarily my favorite, are the bourbon balls and the ultimate pecan turtle. We make seven flavors of caramel, and we dip three of them in chocolate, but on request, we'll dip any of the other ones in chocolate, too. We have a lady at Christmas, she orders the raspberry raisin caramel dipped in white chocolate to be included in her gift boxes she gives away.

Part 4

Celebration Sweets

Shaker Lemon Pie

What is Shaker cooking? Basically it is plain, wholesome food well prepared.

—*Sister Frances Carr,* Shaker Your Plate: Of Shaker Cooks
and Cooking *(1985)*

*T*he United Society of Believers in Christ's Second Appearing is a religious sect more commonly known as Shakers, deriving their name from the practice of "shaking" and dancing during religious services. They have contributed to the world of music through more than ten thousand songs, hymn and anthems, and their style of furniture is sought after and coveted the world over for its simplicity and functionality.

The Shakers of Pleasant Hill in Mercer County, Kentucky, were active from the middle of the Kentucky Revival (a period of spiritual awakening across the state) in 1805 until their dissolution in 1910. The Kentucky Shakers were well known for their culinary skills and industriousness, selling their preserves, baked goods and produce at farmers' markets and trading posts across the South. Their thirty-three buildings and twenty-two miles of dry stone fences on three thousand acres still stand today in the rolling foothills of central Kentucky and attract thousands of hungry tourists each year.

While the Shakers primarily only used ingredients and goods grown on their compound, their key dessert, Shaker Lemon Pie, broke the trend, using lemons that were brought in from the South on the Kentucky River.

COMMUNITY SPOTLIGHT: SHAKERS AND SUSTAINABILITY

What does a community that couldn't even sustain its own populations (they were celibate) know about sustainability? Quite a bit, actually.

The Kentucky Shakers were highly skilled farmers, practicing sustainable agriculture far before the concept had a name. Growing, harvesting and eating were spiritual activities for the Shakers, and they were devoted—almost above all else—to not wasting anything or depending on the outside world for their sustenance.

The Shakers grew and produced enough to feed themselves and then sell to neighbors, in addition to flexing their entrepreneurial muscles through operating one of the largest noncommercial seed businesses in the region. They also were staunch about nutrition, using herbs for flavorings in meals and rejecting the fatty, starchy diet popular during their era for one with a greater focus on locally grown fruits and vegetables and whole grains.

SPOTLIGHT TOOL:
BEEHIVE OVENS

An oven shaped like the hive of everyone's favorite honey-loving insect? While they may not be used exclusively for sweet-and-sticky desserts, the dome-shaped beehive oven is a centuries-old tradition in the United States used extensively by Shakers for baking, roasting and preserving fruits and vegetables.

The use of beehive ovens dates back to the Middle Ages, when they were a fixture of almost every colonial home in America. The ovens were quite roomy, measuring about twelve feet wide, and were heated by preparing a fire several hours in advance from local woods—such as the Kentucky coffeetree or oak—mixed with saplings and scrub brush. The ovens were originally included as part of the hearth in the central part of the house, but they were eventually moved to the side of the hearth so as to not mix food and soot. Beehive ovens were later built outside as stand-alone entities—fully realizing their whimsical shape. They remained popular until the advent of gas and electric ranges, which proved to be time saving and more efficient for home cooks.

The heat in beehive ovens was tested by hand, due to the lack of temperature measurements on the rustic appliance. When creating breads and pies, bakers would hold their hand in the oven for an "eight count" to see if the oven was hot enough. If a baker could hold his or her hand in the over for longer than eight seconds, the oven was not yet hot enough.

Beehive ovens are particularly good for baking pies and breads because of their even heating, especially from the bottom, where pies often end up soggy. The different parts of the beehive ovens were used for baking or cooking different items, with pies being baked most frequently in the front of the oven along with cakes and breads to ensure that they were exposed to the most heat possible. Pies were also some of the first items to bake once the oven heated because they proved to be quite a bit more temperamental.

TIPS AND TRICKS

Paper Thin: Perhaps the most important step of all is to get those lemon slices paper thin—not construction paper thin, not legal paper thin, but tissue paper thin. If you're not scared of blades and have a steady hand, using a mandoline is perhaps the best way to achieve this translucent status.

No Mandoline Mishaps: Patience is a virtue when using this kitchen tool and may save you a lot of blood loss and a trip to the emergency room. When slicing lemons for the pie, remember to tuck your fingers so as to not accidentally expose them to the blade. When you reach the bottom of the mandoline when slicing, use the heel of your hand to push. No matter how tempting it may be, never slice anything without the hand guard, lest you lose the top part of a thumb or finger. If you really want to double up on safety, wear a Kevlar glove (available at most hardware and home good stores) as well when slicing.

SIDEKICK RECIPE SPOTLIGHT: SWEETMEATS

Although the name might sound like a dish of bacon covered in brown sugar or a steak decorated with frosting, sweetmeats is an Appalachian term once used to describe all cakes, pies, pastries and candies in general. Over the years, the term began to find its niche as a name for candied fruits crystalized with honey or sugar, as well as a variety of preserves. This method of candying fruits and nuts also allowed them to last longer, with the sugar acting as a saccharine preservative. (Side note: It would also be a really great, if not a little odd, term of endearment for a loved one.)

Pickled Grapes

Yield: 8 pints

8 cups light brown sugar	½ cup allspice
2 quarts wine vinegar	½ cup ground cinnamon
½ cup cloves	16 cups stemmed half-ripe grapes

In a heavy-bottom saucepan, combine sugar, vinegar and spices. Cook over medium heat, uncovered, for 10–15 minutes, or until the liquid thickens enough to coat the back of a spoon. Divide grapes among eight clean jars, pour warm syrup over them and stir. Allow mixture to marinate for 72 hours. Eat immediately or save in a cool, dry place for up to 3 weeks.

Bonus: If you are interested in canning these instead of eating in the near future, sterilize the jar for 5 minutes in boiling water prior to adding grapes, then sterilize—with lid sealed—for 20 minutes after adding vinegar mixture.

SIDEKICK RECIPE
LEMON ROSEWATER SQUARES

Yield: 24 squares
Active Time: 20 minutes * Total Time: 40 minutes
Special Tools: 9x13-inch baking dish

For the Crust:

½ cup confectioners' sugar

2 cups all-purpose flour

¼ teaspoon salt

2 sticks unsalted butter, softened

1½ tablespoons rosewater

For the Filling:

4 eggs, beaten

2 cups granulated sugar

6 teaspoons lemon juice

1 lemon, zested

¼ cup all-purpose flour

½ teaspoon baking powder

For the Crust:

Preheat the oven to 350°F. Grease pan generously and line with parchment paper. Using a food processor, combine all crust ingredients, pulsing until crumbly. Press the mixture evenly into the bottom of the pan and prick for ventilation. Bake for 20 minutes, until the edges of the crust are golden brown.

For the Filling:

In a large mixing bowl, combine eggs, sugar, lemon juice and lemon zest, whisking until blended. Sift the flour and baking powder over the top of this mixture and mix until completely combined. Pour the filling over the crust and bake until the filling is set and a toothpick inserted in the middle comes out clean, about 20 minutes. Cool and dust with additional powdered sugar, if desired. Serve immediately.

SHAKER LEMON PIE

Yield: 1 9-inch pie (8 servings)
Active Time: 1 hour * Total Time: 2 hours
Special Tools: mandoline

For the Crust:
1 cup all-purpose flour
¼ cup granulated sugar
1 teaspoon salt
1½ teaspoons water, chilled
8 tablespoons lard, chilled

For the Filling:
3 lemons, thinly sliced
2¾ cups granulated sugar
4 large eggs, room temperature
1½ teaspoons kosher salt

For the Crust:

Preheat oven to 350°F. Using a food processor, pulse together flour, sugar, salt, water and lard until the dough pulls away from the sides of the mixer and easily forms a ball. Press the dough into a pie plate. Prick crust with a fork, insert pie weights and parbake crust until golden brown, about 7 minutes.

For the Filling:

Beginning the night before, slice the lemons as thinly as possible using a mandoline, removing the seeds with a knife as you go. Place the slices in a medium bowl and mix gently with 2 cups of granulated sugar. Refrigerate overnight.

Whisk eggs in a medium bowl with ¾ cup of sugar and salt until completely combined. Place a fine layer of lemons on the bottom of the pie crust flush with the sides and circling in. Pour egg mixture over lemon slices. Bake for 1 hour, rotating the pie halfway through, or until the edges are a golden brown. The pie should be allowed to rest for 1–2 hours and is delicious as a breakfast treat the next day.

Hummingbird Cake

*T*his light, fruity cake—which took home top prize at the Kentucky State Fair in 1978—has become a staple of southern cuisine, is rumored to have mysterious Jamaican roots and is a go-to springtime picnic favorite. The blue ribbon–winning recipe from Helen Wiser has gone on to become the most requested recipe in the history of *Southern Living*, the quintessential southern magazine, and raised the profile for subtropical ingredients in southern cooking.

KENTUCKY STATE FAIR: TOP CAKES OF THE DECADE

Is the state fair a good place to judge sugary trends? Perhaps so. Over the past few decades, some noticeable similarities among the annual winning cakes in the "favorite cake" category have raised a few "correlation versus causation" debates among the more analytical sugar lovers. While there are individual categories dedicated to bakeoffs for specific cake types (carrot cake, jam cake, hummingbird cake), the favorite cake category is the real place for bakers to peacock about, strutting their stuff. Was there something about tropical cakes in the 1980s? Are we all about caramel now? What's going to be the next trend? See for yourself. (Hint: It's not chocolate.)

> 2009: Neapolitan (Chocolate, Vanilla, Strawberry) Party Cake
> 2010: Raspberry Red Velvet Cake with Chocolate Ganache Filling and Vanilla Bean Frosting
> 2011: Brown Sugar Walnut Caramel Cake
> 2012: Autumn Memories (Banana, Black Walnuts, Coconut) Cake
> 2013: Chocolate Raspberry Cake

SPOTLIGHT INGREDIENT: PINEAPPLE

Straight from the exotic fruit files, here's a shocking reveal: pineapples have actually been a part of cargoes coming from the Caribbean to North America since the late eighteenth century, when they were a precious commodity among settlers in the Virginia colonies. A lack of canning and preservation technologies, though, made its presence reserved for special occasions and holidays until the turn of the twentieth century. The United States' 1898 annexation of Hawaii—the state now synonymous with this good luck fruit—after the Spanish-American War and the arrival of an upstart businessman with an eye for advertising, James Dole, allowed pineapple to begin its ascent to mass popularity, where it quickly became a staple in homes across the United States and a key ingredient in celebration cakes.

Hummingbird Cake Aliases
Jamaica cake, doctor bird cake, granny cake, cake that don't last

COMMUNITY SPOTLIGHT: COMMUNITY COOKBOOKS

Long before the advent of Pinterest and Foodspotting, women across Kentucky were swapping recipes and compiling cooking tips through organizational and community cookbooks. Community cookbooks were primarily published by churches and local social leagues to raise funds for projects or charity work but also as a means of reinforcing local pride and ensuring that heritage recipes were passed down to posterity. The depth and breadth of community cookbooks in Kentucky affords it one of the most robust collections of local recipe books in the country, celebrating not only regional variations on Kentucky classics but also hyper-local favorites from across the state.

Must-Have 100+-Year-Old Kentucky Cookbooks

The Kentucky Housewife, Lettice Bryan (1839)
The Blue Grass Cookbook, Minnie Fox (1904)
The Blue Ribbon Cookbook, Jennie C. Benedict (1904)

SIDEKICK COCKTAIL CREAMY COCONUT

Yield: 4 servings

¼ cup dark rum
¼ cup tequila
I cup coconut cream
I cup coconut water
¼ cup lime juice
4 pineapple wedges, garnish

Pulse all ingredients, minus pineapple wedges, until smooth in a blender. Pour into glass, garnish with pineapple wedges.

TIPS AND TRICKS

Egghead: There are many times when home cooks wonder if they can cut corners when baking. Do I really have to use cake flour? (Yes.) Isn't vanilla extract the same thing as vanilla bean? (No.) One of these potentially-going-to-break-the-rules conundrums is whether to use the exact size of egg that's called for in a recipe. The answer? An unequivocal yes. While it may seem tedious, it's very important to use the correct size of egg for which the recipe calls. Using extra-large eggs in the place of large will add unnecessary liquid to your baked good, potentially making it too wet. Not convinced? Substituting four extra-large eggs in a recipe that only calls for four large eggs will add an extra half an egg in volume to your recipe. Yikes. If a recipe doesn't specify, it's safe to assume they think you are using large, or jumbo, eggs.

Ice, Ice Baby: While everyone has their tips and tricks for how to properly ice a layer cake, it's still a daunting task. Let's break it down into manageable bites:

Step One: Most likely, your cake has a slight dome shape at the top. Not to fear. Slice the domed section off using a serrated knife, gently moving back and forth using a sawing motion.

Step Two: Prepare a kitchen plate or cake board roughly 1 inch larger than your cake as the base for your creation. Take a generous dab of frosting and place it in the center of the cake board to ensure that the bottom layer holds steady.

Step Three: Place your bottom cake layer on the board or plate, securing it to the frosting glue. Spoon about ⅓ cup of frosting onto the center of the bottom layer and, using an offset spatula, spread the frosting to the edges of the cake. Repeat frosting, cake, frosting, cake for as many layers as necessary, remembering to use a similar amount of frosting between each layer.

Step Four: Ah, the crumb coat. This is when things usually get a little tricky. Using the offset spatula, apply a thin coat of frosting to the sides and top of the cake. It's totally fine if the cake still shows through, this is just a base coat.

Step Five: Chill your cake in order to set the crumb coat for 45 minutes to an hour.

Step Six: Remove the cake from the refrigerator and ice the top. (Don't worry, we'll smooth it out in a second.) Now comes the hard part. Dollop icing every 2 inches along the outside of the cake, then begin to carefully spread evenly with the offset spatula.

Step Seven: Time to smooth it out. Using a scraper in one hand and rotating the cake with the other, gently smooth the sides of the cake until even. After the sides are properly satiny, smooth the top. Stand back and admire your work.

Hummingbird Cake

Yield: 1 9-inch, 3-layer cake (12–14 servings)
Active Time: 30 minutes * Total Time: 1 hour, 15 minutes
Special Tools: electric handheld mixer, wire cooling rack,
offset spatula, cake stand

For the Cake:

- 3 cups all-purpose flour
- 1 teaspoon baking soda
- ½ teaspoon salt
- 1 cup white sugar
- 1 cup light brown sugar
- 1 teaspoon ground cinnamon
- 1 teaspoon ground ginger
- 3 large eggs
- 1 cup vegetable oil
- 2 teaspoons vanilla extract
- 1 (8-ounce) can crushed pineapple, drained
- 1 cup chopped pecans
- 2 cups ripe bananas, mashed

For the Frosting:

- 1 (8-ounce) package cream cheese, softened
- ½ cup unsalted butter, softened
- 2 cups confectioners' sugar
- 1 teaspoon vanilla extract

For the Cake:
Grease three 9-inch round cake pans generously and preheat oven to 350°F. Sift dry ingredients (flour, baking soda, salt, sugars and spices) together in a large bowl, Add eggs one at a time, stirring after each addition until completely incorporated. Add oil and stir gently until batter is smooth and ribbon-like. Add vanilla, pineapple, pecans and banana, mixing until evenly distributed. Pour batter into prepared cake pans and bake, remembering to rotate cakes halfway through, until edges are golden and a toothpick inserted in the center comes out clean, about 30 minutes.

For the Frosting:
Using a handheld electric mixer, beat cream cheese and butter in a large bowl at medium speed until smooth. Turning the mixer to low, slowly and steadily add powdered sugar, beating until frosting is light and fluffy. Stir in vanilla with a wooden spoon. Once cake has cooled, spread cream cheese frosting between layers and on top and sides of cake. The cake can be stored in an airtight container in the refrigerator for up to five days.

TRANSPARENT PIE

When I was growing up, my grandmother's house was a wonderland of trinkets and tinkering—a place where an early twentieth-century pimento cheese grinder dominated the dining room table, a taxidermy bobcat served as a coffee table and an extensive collection of bird-shaped pie vents perched on the kitchen windowsill, peeping down (in what I assumed to be harsh judgment) at the messes of sugar and lard that I would concoct as a child.

One of the first successful pies I whipped up was transparent pie: a dessert so filled with sugar (two cups!) that I'm sure it has single-handedly bankrolled several area dentists for decades.

SWEET SHOWDOWN:
TRANSPARENT PIE VERSUS CHESS PIE
VERSUS BUTTERMILK PIE

What makes transparent pie different than the old southern standby chess pie? The use of heavy cream. While they may be kissing cousins, the cream adds a level of richness that sets it apart and gives it a smooth, custardy texture. The Texas classic buttermilk pie, which has a tart, tangy bite, also falls into this saccharine family of confections, replacing the heavy cream with buttermilk. The Indiana sugar pie and the rural Pennsylvania favorite shoofly pie also are regional custard pie favorites of a similar ilk. (Little old ladies across the state of Kentucky would shake their heads disparagingly at these comparisons, though, so keep them to a whisper.)

TIPS AND TRICKS

Puff Daddy: When the pie is baking, it will puff up much like a cake. Do not be alarmed when this happens. The pie will sink back down (and many times become a bit concave) once allowed to cool. The pie is ready to be removed from the oven when a crispy, golden brown shell has formed on its top. The shell is deliciously addictive—like a thin sugar cookie—but resist the urge to snap off crisp, sugary bites: it should be allowed to mingle with the creamy center of the pie in each mouthful.

Think Thin: This pie should not be served in regular-sized slices but instead in very thin slivers; it is incredibly rich and is best enjoyed in this delicate form. The pie can either be served warm—perhaps even for breakfast, with a strong cup of black coffee—or kept classic with a chilled slice and a trusty glass of frothy milk.

HISTORICAL SPOTLIGHT: SUGARLOAF

There's no doubt about it—transparent pie is the ultimate sweet tooth dessert. With a pie like that, it's a shame that granulated sugar is no longer packaged in its traditional sugarloaf form. Until the late nineteenth century, sugar was packaged as a conical "loaf" with a rounded top, calling for bakers to cut off hunks of sugar when they needed it for baking. A special set of oddly shaped pliers called "sugar nips" was created specifically for this purpose. The heavier the sugar nips were, the safer the practice of nibbling off bits of sugar. The sugarloaf also became emblematic of a grocer and was frequently displayed in front of grocery shops.

TRANSPARENT PIE

Yield: 1 9-inch pie (8 servings)
Active Time: 20 minutes * Total Time: 1 hour

For the Crust:
1 cup all-purpose flour
¼ cup granulated sugar
1 teaspoon salt
1½ teaspoons water, chilled
8 tablespoons lard, chilled

For the Filling:
8 tablespoons butter, softened
2 cups granulated sugar
1 cup (about 8 ounces) heavy cream
4 medium eggs, beaten
2 tablespoons all-purpose flour
1 teaspoon vanilla extract

For the Crust:
Preheat oven to 350°F. Using a food processor, pulse together flour, sugar, salt, water and lard until the dough pulls away from the sides of the mixer and easily forms a ball. Press the dough into a pie plate. Parbake the empty crust until golden brown, about 10 minutes.

For the Filling:
Using an electric hand mixer or stand mixer fitted with a paddle attachment, beat together butter and sugar until fluffy, about 3 minutes. Add cream and eggs, beating until smooth, then stir in flour and vanilla with a large spatula. Pour filling into crust. Bake until a golden brown crust forms on top, about 40 minutes.

SWEET SOUND OFF:
JUDY DICKSON
CO-OWNER, MAGEE'S BAKERY

The dictionary definition of a family bakery, Magee's in Maysville, Kentucky, is the home of the original transparent pie. Here, co-owner Judy Dickson talks about her decades of experience running a bakery and the surprises she's encountered along the way.

Tell us a little bit about Maysville. Are you from there?

I am from Maysville, and my husband is also from Maysville, right here in Orangeburg. The bakery is located on my home farm—the farm I grew up on. We moved it [Magee's] about ten years ago to the farm that I grew up on so that we could do tours. What we do on our tours is we let people make their own dinner rolls, also stamp out their own tart shells and fill them. When all that's done, they eat the country meal. We have a big country meal of country ham, butter biscuits, scalloped cabbage, corn pudding, roast beef and just anything country. What we try to do is stay within whatever season it is, so if it's spring, whatever's in the gardens in this part of the country, then we have that. If it's midsummer, we have whatever's in the gardens then. If it's in fall, we have the squash and bean soup or whatever is in season.

What were your favorite sweet things to eat growing up?

Well, see, we grew up out here in the country. We went to the store once a week at most, and they got us a bag of candy that we divided among eight children—so it always tastes good no matter what kind of candy. My mother always made jam cake, country things like that. I do like her jam cakes. She always made them with blackberry jam because that's a fruit that grows here in Kentucky. Of course, I always liked apple pie, too, because there's always a lot of apples around.

Magee's has been a Maysville staple for decades. Did you always want to own a bakery?

Magee's was established in 1941. We lived here, but we had a medical problem when our first child was to be born so we had to be close to a hospital in Cincinnati so we could change out blood. We stayed in Cincinnati for eight years, my husband was in the newspaper business, and when we came back here, we saw Magee's was for sale in 1973, so we bought it. We kept the name Magee's.

How is the Magee's in Maysville related to Magee's in other parts of the state?

The original Magee's started here in Maysville. Mrs. Magee owned the original one, the one that we bought, but Mr. Magee owned the others. He didn't start the one in Lexington or the one in Frankfort—it's closed now—until 1956. That's the reason that we stuck with the original recipes and everything. We've never changed from the original recipes ever. We're the ones that made the transparent pie famous. We're on a lot of Kentucky bucket lists.

When did you first taste transparent pie? What was your first thought?

I was probably maybe ten years old before I tasted transparent. My Aunt Mary made it. I thought, "This is the best thing I've ever tasted in my life!" As children, we had manners—they taught us manners. You ate one, and that's all you ate. I would've taken ten of them if I could've, but I know I was only to take that one and that's all I took.

Are you a filling person or a crust person?

I like the crust, because ours are still homemade crusts. The people who eat it like pudding like the filling; the ones who eat it like a tart are the crust folks. It was originally called pudding because if they didn't have the ingredients for the pie crust, they just had a pudding made out of the filling. Transparent pie was originally poor man's pie because on farms, everything that's in it you could walk out onto the farm and get—eggs, milk, sugar cane, flour—everything in it.

Do people call and request both pies and puddings, even though it's the same dish?

Yes, we send them all over the United States. We mail them.

Tell me a little bit about the transparent pie and how it's made.

We have our own formula, where we make the homemade shells first and then mix up the filling according to our formula. We make about fifty dozen pies every day. The day before Christmas last year, when we finally cut it off with the mailman, we sent out eighty-one dozen that last day. Some days we'd send out forty-five dozen or even twenty-five dozen, but that last day when we said, "We're not doing anymore!" everybody rushed their orders in that day. Some boxes even had more than a dozen in them!

Tell us how transparent pie got its own festival. What are some of the activities?

We just decided that we'd come back to the community where we were raised, and we wanted to have something for the community, so we had it. Now, we don't have that anymore because my husband had a bad heart attack. It's a lot of work to put on a festival. The neighbors always would bring their horses and wagons, and they all got older, too. We did for the first seven years after we moved back to the farm in Orangeburg. As everyone got older and got health problems, we just kind of quit because the younger people just aren't into that. We had tractor rides and everything.

I know transparent pie has some celebrity admirers. Could you tell us a little bit more about that?

Well, of course, our main one right now is George Clooney. Another kid that grew up in the bakery and our kids ran around with was Miss America 2000, Heather Renee French. So, we've had a lot of help in promoting and have been able to meet a lot of celebrities through that like Bob Hope, Barbara Walters and so forth. A lot of them have been with Rosemary, Nick and Nina through the years.

What's the most exciting event that's happened in Magee's?

A wedding! These two people came in, and it seemed they were planning on getting married in Fleming County. The families got in it, though, and said, "Oh, we want it this way! We want it that way! Do this! Do that!" So, the kids just came into the bakery one day and said, "Do you know where we can get a preacher?" We started calling around to see but couldn't raise a preacher on a Saturday afternoon for anything. We knew the county judge who was out on his farm, so we called his wife and asked for his cellphone number. Well, she said, "Don't tell him I gave this to you!" but in about twenty minutes, he was there. My husband and I stood up with them, fixed them a little cake and told customers as they came in, "Now just stand over there in a corner, we're having a little wedding right now!" The bride asked one customer if she'd take pictures, so they had an instant photographer, instant couple to stand up with them, and the judge married them and they're still together today. They're in Morehead now, I think.

What are some of the other sweets that Magee's is known for?

Everyone loves our cream horns, of course; we sell a world of those. We also are known for our cake squares, which is butter cake with a white icing—that was one of Rosemary Clooney's favorite things. She liked jam cake, cake squares and transparent pie. Now, we don't do doughnuts because we're so busy with the big items we just can't do sweet rolls and all that.

If transparent pie had a theme song, what would it be?

[Judy, laughing]: Oh, lordy. You ask Russ that question; he'll have a good answer for it!

[Russ]: Okay, let me go for it. When we first moved out here, we played, "Country Road" by John Denver, so I guess that's kind of the theme song to the bakery and this pie.

SIDEKICK LIQUOR
LIMONCELLO

Yield: 2.5 liters

10 organic lemons
1 bottle of (high-quality) 100-proof
  vodka

1½ cups water
1¼ cups sugar

Zest all lemons, collecting zest in a small bowl. Set lemons aside. Pour the zest in an airtight dark glass container and add vodka, stirring to combine. Seal the mixture and let it steep in a cool, dark place for at least three weeks.

After three weeks, create a simple syrup by bringing water and sugar to a boil in a heavy-bottom saucepan over high heat. Remove from heat and allow syrup to cool. Once cooled, pour into lemon mixture, stir well and allow the new mixture to sit for a minimum of 72 hours. Filter the mixture through a sieve into a clean glass bowl, removing the lemon zest. Next, place a coffee filter in the sieve. Pour limoncello through the coffee filter. Ladle into a clean glass bottle. Serve immediately or store in refrigerator indefinitely.

SIDEKICK RECIPE
CANDIED LEMON PEEL

Yield: ½ cup candied peel

1 large (preferably organic) lemon
7 cups cold water
2½ cups granulated sugar

Use a vegetable peeler to remove lemon peel, taking as much of the skin as possible and avoiding the white pith. Set lemon aside. Combine the peel with 2 cups cold water in a heavy-bottom saucepan, bring to a boil and then drain. Repeat this process twice more, on the third time removing the peels and laying on a cool, dry surface. Take 2 cups of sugar and add to saucepan with 1 cup water, whisking until sugar dissolves. Add the peels and bring to a boil. Once boiling for 1–2 minutes, reduce heat and simmer, uncovered, until the peels are tender and translucent, about 15 minutes. Drain the peels and spread out on a cool, dry surface. Add the remaining ½ cup sugar into a medium bowl along with cooled peels and toss to coat. Remove the peels one at a time using a fork, gently shaking each to remove excess sugar. Store in an airtight container for up to five weeks.

SPOTLIGHT: MERINGUE

There's something inherently magical about meringue. This fluffy, delicate dessert (and dessert accessory) is a testament to how the science—and simplicity—of sweets can seem almost unreal. Meringue has always been something of the mysterious, intimidating, quasi-European (is it French? Maybe Italian?) dessert of the sweet world—that girl who always seems so effortlessly ethereal at parties that you want to be bitter about it, but she's just so darn sweet you can't bring yourself to do it.

While many assume that the French were the originators of meringue, *pas si*. The credit for the first iteration of the dessert goes to two Englishwomen, who defied the odds of their time (reading and writing were not, ahem, "ladylike") and secured a solid place in international culinary history. Lady Elinor Fettiplace of Appleton in Berkshire (now Oxfordshire) recorded the first baked beaten-egg-white-and-sugar confection in a manuscript book in 1604. The handwritten recipe for "white bisket bread" is comparable to the fluffy confection we know and love today. After her death, the book was passed down to her niece and published under the title *Elinor Fettiplace's Receipt Book—Elizabethan Country House Cooking*. In 1630, Lady Rachel Fane of Knole, Kent, recorded an almost identical recipe for "pets" using the same preparation and ingredients as Lady Fettiplace's creations. Although they lived and baked in roughly the same era, there are no records to indicate that the two women knew each other or ever corresponded. Thus is the divine magic of meringue.

Meanwhile in France, King Louis XIV's first chef, François Massialot, is responsible for coining the word *meringue* when he published a recipe for a baked beaten-egg-white-and-sugar confection in his 1692 cookbook. The book was translated into English in 1702, and the citation in the Oxford English Dictionary for the first use of the term came shortly thereafter in 1706.

While there are many legends about how a Swiss chef is perhaps the originator of the meringue recipe in 1720, they have largely been debunked over the years as the layered history of our favorite fluffy confection has been peeled back one layer at a time.

TIPS AND TRICKS

Keep It Chilly: The key word when making your pâte brisee is to keep it cold—ice cold. The colder the butter can be (frozen, not just refrigerated) and the chillier you can keep your hands (running them under ice water isn't a terrible idea), the flakier and tenderer your pie crust will turn out. If your crust seems to be getting too warm or sticky, let it rest in the refrigerator for 10–15 minutes to give the gluten time to calm down.

Bowled Over: Use a metal or glass—preferably copper—mixing bowl when beating your egg whites for the greatest volume. Fats are easily left clinging to the sides of plastic mixing bowls, which inhibits the volume of the egg whites.

How's the Weather: While it can't be entirely avoided (and if you live in certain areas, it's impossible), try to bake your pie on a day that has relatively low humidity. The sticky air will make the sugars in the meringue chewy and might alter cooking time.

Don't Peak Too Soon: There are several stages egg whites go through on their way to becoming a meringue. (You have to crawl before you can walk, you know.) For the pie topping, soft peaks are acceptable, but stiff peaks are the desired texture. Here's how to identify them in a lineup:

Soft Peaks: The peaks can form if coaxed but melt back down in seconds— soft and fluffy.

Firm Peaks: The peaks are matte but firm and smooth. You can curl the peaks, but they won't stand on their own.

Stiff Peaks: The peaks are glossy and stiff enough to cut, standing up easily on their own.

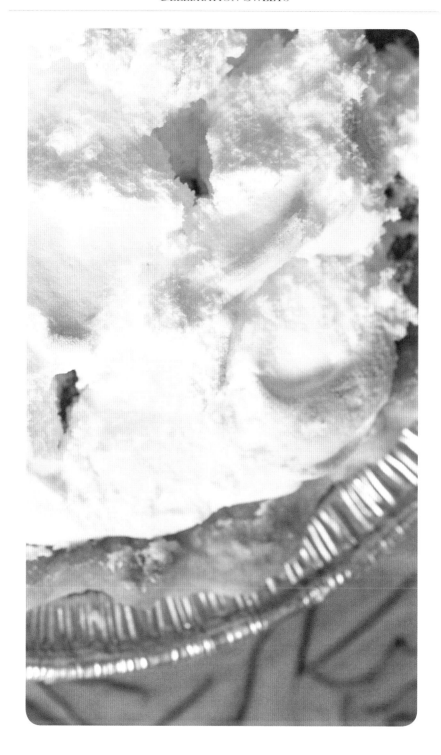

MILE HIGH LEMON MERINGUE PIE

Yield: 1 9-inch pie
Active Time: 30 minutes * Total Time: 2 hours, 30 minutes

For the Crust:
1½ cups all-purpose
   flour
4 tablespoons
   granulated sugar
½ teaspoon salt
6 tablespoons unsalted
   butter, chilled and
   cubed
1 large egg yolk
3–4 tablespoons ice
   water

For the Filling:
⅓ cup cornstarch
1¼ cups granulated
   sugar
⅔ cup all-purpose
   flour, sifted
½ cup lemon juice
2 cups water
5 egg yolks
3 tablespoons lemon
   zest
5 tablespoons unsalted
   butter, chilled and
   cubed

For the Meringue:
6 large egg whites
¾ cup granulated sugar

For the Crust:

Combine flour, sugar and salt in a food processor and blend. Add butter and pulse until the mixture is crumbly and coarse, about 15 seconds. Add egg yolk slowly to the mixture and pulse for 15 more seconds, or until the dough begins to pull away from the sides of the processor. Add ice water, 1 tablespoon at a time, until the dough holds together without being sticky. Remove the dough, form into two 1-inch discs and refrigerate for a minimum of 1 hour. The extra crust can be kept for up to 1 month in the freezer.

For the Filling:

Preheat oven to 400°F. On a lightly floured surface, roll one dough disc until $1/8$ inch thick and press into pie plate. Prick bottom of the shell with a fork, fill with pie weights and parbake until crust is golden brown, about 20 minutes.

While crust is baking, combine cornstarch, sugar, flour, lemon juice and water in a medium heavy-bottom saucepan over medium heat. Bring to a boil, whisking constantly, until mixture turns translucent and shiny, about 3 minutes. Remove pan from heat and whisk in egg yolks one at a time. Return saucepan to low heat and whisk in lemon zest and butter. Pour mixture into a medium-sized bowl set over a tray of cold water and let cool. Once filling is cooled, pour into prepared crust and refrigerate until set, about 2 hours.

For Meringue:

In a large metal bowl, whisk egg whites until foamy. Slowly stream in sugar until stiff peaks begin to form. Pour meringue on top of prepared pie and spread evenly. Broil until brown, about 1 minute. Serve immediately at room temperature. The pie will keep for up to two days, but it is best served on the day of creation.

SWEET SOUND OFF:
MICHAEL TULLAR
OWNER, PATTI'S 1880S SETTLEMENT
GRAND RIVERS, KENTUCKY

Grand Rivers sits in the middle of a water wonderland in the western part of the state. Aside from the hunting, the fishing and the Fancy Farm picnic (everyone's favorite political weekend), the area's main attraction is Patti's 1880s Settlement. Patti's is not just a restaurant, although it boasts a robust menu of meats, sides and candies. This sprawling destination locale is a compound filled with entertainment, shopping and the kitschy, old-timey charm of a rustic Disneyland. One of its most renowned signature desserts is its massively tall, robust lemon meringue pie.

Tell me a little bit about how Patti's came to be. Are you from Grand Rivers?
Actually, my parents moved all around. My parents met in Arizona during the war, World War II, and my dad was out there in the hospital. My mom went to visit the gentleman in the next bed over in the hospital, but they got to talking, then started dating and eventually got married and had us. They then moved to California, then to Hawaii, where we lived for six years, then my parents ended up in western Kentucky. My mother talked my oldest brother into coming back and opening up a hamburger stand, which was called Hamburger Patti's Ice Cream Parlor, in 1977. That was the beginning. Then I came back in 1982 from California with the promise of a lot of hunting and fishing and boating and water skiing and all these recreational activities we have around here. Some of the features that come from what we've created here at Patti's are from all over. Our flowerpot bread comes from my mother baking bread in clay pots like the Indians in the Southwest, and some of our flavorings come from the Hawaiian Islands, California—a lot of different backgrounds being brought together. It's a lot different than the normal southern cooking spot.

Is there any reason y'all chose to make a lemon meringue pie? Is it a family recipe?
My mom and my brother realized that they had to make something different to set themselves apart from every place else. That's how they came up with our most famous meat dish, too. My mom went to the butcher and said, "I want a great big pork chop. Give me one that's two inches thick." So the local butcher started cutting her two-inch-thick pork chops. At first, we

stuffed them and baked them, until one night when they ran out of stuffed chopped. A hunter who was in said, "Just cook me one, I don't care how you do it!" So they put it on the charbroiler, and that was the beginning of how we started cooking the two-inch chops.

The pies and stuff are just family recipes, but what sets our lemon meringue pie apart is that it averages about twelve egg whites per pie in the meringue. The meringue stands on average six to eight inches off of the pie, some taller. The rest of it is really cooking to taste and making sure everyone really enjoys it before you put it on a menu.

About how many pies would you say you serve a year?
Oh, gosh. I'd have to do that math. I'd guess about ten to twenty thousand, maybe even more. They probably make fifty or sixty pies in one day. We have seventeen desserts that are on our menu pretty much at all times.

Who are the people who come to Patti's?
It's a combination of a lot of different folks who come through all the time. In the fall, you have hunters, and in the spring, you have a lot of fishermen coming down to the lakes. In summertime, lots of families traveling through and meeting at the lakes to have family reunions. The winter months, we have 700,000 Christmas lights, and [the] place is just decorated to the max, and it's so beautiful that the place is absolutely packed.

Could you talk a little bit about the Patti's compound?
Back in the 1980s, we had one Patti's Restaurant, and we had a gift shop on the end of it. My grandmother would run the gift shop, and she was blind, but she knew the prices to everything and she'd ring it up. Of course, she'd make a mistake every once in a while. The food kept getting better, and we started losing people because everyone was coming and the wait was so long to get a table. In the early 1990s, we built Mr. Bill's side on as a place for bus tours, giving them another option or place to go. When we first opened that restaurant, it had honky-tonk piano players, and the ladies were dressed in saloon outfits, but we had two honky-tonk piano players have heart attacks and pass away on us, so that gradually finished that portion of Mr. Bill's. Everyone continued to want the big pork chop and lemon pie and everything that was on the Patti's side of the restaurant, so eventually it just turned into another dining room of Patti's. So, now both places can be filled up at one time, and we can do 2,100 people on a Saturday, or this past December, we did over 41,000 people. It's not bad for a town of 350 people.

Are there any famous faces who have visited?

We know all the politicians across the state, and they stop by quite a bit. We had Demi Moore and Bruce Willis in one time, and when folks were in the area filming *The Fugitive*, they all came in and ate for a couple of weeks. We've had a lot of country western stars come around and others, but really the Bruce Willis one was nice.

Favorite event?

The Christmas lighting ceremony is my favorite part of the year. For the past eight or nine years, we have a huge lighting ceremony the second Friday night in November. We've been having a gospel group called the Eternal Vision come and sing every time, and they do a marvelous job. We usually get two or three hundred people lined up around the big gazebo out back, and they sing and tell jokes, then we turn the lights off as people are arriving and usher people around with flashlights. At 6:00 p.m., we introduce my garden crew and different members of the business who had put up all the Christmas lights, and then we start flipping all the timers and relays on. It lights up! The whole evening, everyone is *oohing* and *ahhing*, walking around enjoying themselves. That's pretty special.

ORANGE BLOSSOM BREAD

***O**nce used as a perfume and aromatic for the home by the upper crust of Louisville and Lexington in the Victorian era, orange blossom evokes the feeling of the exotic and magical whether inhaled, imbibed or ingested.*

How to Wrap Quick Breads in a Tea Towel

Quick breads, such as this orange blossom bread, are a fantastic hostess gift and are particularly charming when wrapped in a tea towel. The bread will be delicious, and the tea towel will remind the lucky recipient of your overwhelming Kentucky hospitality.

loaf of quick bread
parchment paper
tea towel
scotch tape
twine/ribbon

Wrap loaf of bread in parchment paper. Place bread in center of kitchen towel. Bring both sides up and fold down. Fold ends under loaf of bread and secure with scotch tape. Wrap ribbon around bread and secure with more scotch tape. Arrange flower embellishments and gift tag and secure with scotch tape.

TIPS AND TRICKS

Too Cool: Store orange blossom water in a cool, dark place, and it will keep for up to 90 days. If not stored under these conditions, the water will begin to ferment and smell like moth balls (very unappetizing).

Additional Uses for Orange Blossom Water
room scent, bath fragrance, hand freshener, perfume, added to lemonade, salad dressing, added to honey, added to sparkling water

SIDEKICK COCKTAIL
ORANGE BLOSSOM SANGRIA

Yield: 6–8 servings

1 bottle white wine
1¼ cups pear juice
¼ cup orange blossom water
1 cup white grapes, halved
1 cup raspberries, washed and dried
2 blood oranges, peeled and diced

Combine all ingredients and stir well. Refrigerate until the sangria is chilled and the flavors have blended, stirring on the hour, about 3 hours. Pour the sangria into old-fashioned glasses and serve immediately.

ORANGE BLOSSOM BREAD

Yield: 2 9x13-inch loaves (10–12 servings)
Active Time: 20 minutes * Total Time: 50 minutes

For the Bread:

1 cup unsalted butter, chilled

5 cups self-rising flour

2 navel oranges, zested

½ cup granulated sugar

4 tablespoons orange blossom water (see following section)

2 cups whole milk

½ cup pecans, finely chopped

For the Glaze:

1 cup butter

¾ cup granulated sugar

1 teaspoon orange blossom water

1 tablespoon orange extract

For the Bread:

Preheat oven to 350°F and grease loaf pans. Combine butter and flour in food processor, pulsing until the dough begins to pull away from the sides. Remove dough and place in a large, well-oiled bowl. Make a small well in the center. Combine orange zest, sugar and orange blossom water in a small bowl and stir. Add orange mixture and milk to the center of the well. Fold together with a wooden spoon until completely combined. Fold in pecans. The dough should be moist and shiny.

Remove dough from bowl, and on a well-floured surface, knead using the heels of your floured hands 3–4 times. Divide the dough in half and place in loaf pans.

For the Glaze:

In a small saucepan, melt butter over medium heat, then whisk in sugar, stirring consistently until completely combined. Remove from heat and add orange blossom water and orange extract. Pour glaze over dough and bake until brown around the edges, about 30 minutes. The bread can be eaten immediately, wrapped and saved for up to four days or frozen for up to two months.

How to Make Orange Blossom Water

Orange blossom water should be readily available at any specialty store or holistic market. In the event that it's completely unavailable or you want to make your own, here's a handy guide.

It is impossible to grow oranges in Kentucky. Sorry, folks. Order petals of the orange tree (preferably the Seville or bitter orange) online, ensuring that the plants or plant offspring that you will be receiving are both bug and pesticide free. Rinse the petals and blossom carefully in cold water. Crush the petals with a mortar and pestle and place them in a jar with 2 cups of distilled water. Show some restraint when initially adding petals— you can always up the flavor, but you can't take it away. Leave the jar, with the lid on, in the sun for a few weeks and check the scent. If it is too weak, continue to leave in the sun for another week or so.

ALE-8 BUNDT CAKE

*A*le-8-One—known colloquially as "Ale-8"—has been bottled in Winchester, Kentucky, since 1926 and a household staple for almost ninety years. Winchester, a small town located just east of Lexington, teeters on the edge of horse country and Appalachia, and the fusion of culinary traditions from the two regions can be found in the unique flavor of the soda. While the exact recipe is a closely guarded secret known only by descendants of the company's eccentric founder, G.L. Wainscott, it's no secret that ginger is at the heart of the drink's spicy appeal—it is lighter than a typical ginger ale but with a punch more akin to a full-bodied ginger beer. Wild ginger is not only a popular flavoring agent for meals in eastern Kentucky but also well known as a folk medicine cure for everything from hangovers to teething pains in babies. The citrus notes that pepper the drink speak to the era of the soda's creation, when oranges and lemons were rare treats only available in larger cities such as Lexington and Louisville.

While the first bottling plant was a small operation located in an old livery stable, the company has seen tremendous longevity, going on to become Kentucky's only still-active native soda. The curious name can be traced back to Mr. Wainscott's role as a man ahead of his time: the company hosted a nationwide slogan contest—one of the first in the United States—to find just the right name for the sweet new concoction. Ale-8-One ("A Late One") won the day as a name that set apart the soda as the latest to come on the market.

Any church cakewalk or school bake sale in central Kentucky will undoubtedly have a sweet ode to Ale-8 as an offering. The Ale-8 Bundt cake, topped with an extra helping of soda in the cake's glaze, gives a traditional pound cake a truly Kentucky touch.

SPOTLIGHT:
SOUTHERN REGIONAL SODAS

While Coca-Cola may reign supreme across the region, locally branded and bottled sodas are a serious source of pride south of the Mason-Dixon line. Kentucky's native beverage is assuredly not left out of the soda shuffle, as Ale-8-One has acquired a devoted fan base spanning not only across the state but also the globe—any expatriated Kentuckian will assuredly request a six-pack of the frothy drink in a care package from home. Here are a few others.

Dr. Enuf: Few soft drinks attempt to pass themselves off as health products, but Dr. Enuf's vitamin- and mineral-fortified bubbles might actually be able to cut the medicinal mustard. Bottled in Johnson City, Tennessee, by the same company originally responsible for Mountain Dew, Dr. Enuf has a fizzy, lemon-lime flavor with an herbal kick at the end that, reputedly, helps to cure hangovers.

Grapico: Alabama's very own grape soda, Grapico, has been produced in the state since moving there from its original New Orleans hub in 1917. A thick, syrupy soda with a highly concentrated grape flavor, it was a favorite of Fannie Flagg's heroine in the classic novel *Fried Green Tomatoes at the Whistle Stop Café*. Grapico has also inspired a cocktail dubiously called "The Ex-Girlfriend," which combines the grape-flavored drink with jalapeño vodka.

Cheerwine: Founded in 1917, North Carolina's Cheerwine is known for its rich cherry flavor and lays claim to the fact that it is the oldest soda continuously produced by the same family. The deep burgundy color of the drink and its high amount of carbonation make it unique among soft drinks. Each year, the soda hosts an annual competition to elect an official "Miss Cheerwine" ambassador, who represents the company at events and festivals across the country. While the company is largely associated with the Old North State, Cheerwine was originally founded in Maysville, Kentucky, but it relocated when the owners went bankrupt.

Tool Spotlight: Bundt Cake Pan

While Bundt cake pans are par for the course in kitchens throughout the United States today, few inquiring minds stop to ask quite why this pan's popularity is so widespread. After all,

what about the madeleine pan? Or the Finish savarin pan? What makes this ring-shaped mold, with its decorative fluted shape and cake-hollowing chimney center, so appealing?

The original Bundt cakes were staple dishes in Germany, Austria and Hungary called *bundkuchen*, stemming from the German word *bund*, which refers to a gathering of people or celebration, and *kuchen*, the German word for cake. (In short, Bundt cakes have always been party cakes.)

After returning from World War II, Minnesota native Henry David Dalquist, founder of the kitchenware company Nordic Ware (also famous for the patented Micro-Go-Round, better known as the automated food rotator inside microwaves), began making Bundt pans in response to requests from members of the Hadassah Society, a Jewish group of women who wanted to make cakes they remembered growing up with in Europe.

The pan sold rather poorly until 1966, when a Bundt cake called the "Tunnel of Fudge" took second place at the annual Pillsbury Bakeoff and won $5,000. More than 200,000 requests for the pan filtered in quickly, eventually surpassing the tin Jell-O mold as the most sought-after pan in the United Sates.

The Bundt cake is one of a handful of confections that derives its name not specifically from its ingredients or recipe but rather from its shape. The majority of Bundt cakes, however, are thick and dense, akin to pound cakes.

Several of the original Bundt pans produced by Dalquist are part of the Smithsonian's collection in Washington, D.C.

SIDEKICK DRINK
THE KENTUCKY COCKTAIL

Yield: 1 cocktail

1½ ounces Kentucky bourbon
½ ounce grenadine
4 ounces Ale-8-One
maraschino cherry, to garnish

Fill rocks glass with ice. Pour bourbon into glass, followed by grenadine and Ale-8-One. Garnish with a maraschino cherry.

TIPS AND TRICKS

Easy, Greasy: Greasing a Bundt pan can be a tricky endeavor because of all the nooks and crannies therein. In order to ensure that your Bundt cakes never stick, melt 2 tablespoons of butter and use a pastry brush to apply the butter to the inside of the pan. The pastry brush allows you to get the butter into the hard-to-reach crevices of the pan. The two areas that will need the most attention are the bottom of the pan, which has the nuanced curves, and where the tube meets the bottom, which sticks most often when trying to remove the cake. The traditional method of softening butter, however, tends to coat these pans unevenly—thickly in some spots and missing others entirely. Flouring the pan after a good coat of butter is extra anti-sticking insurance.

ALE-8 BUNDT CAKE

Yield: 1 12-cup Bundt cake (10–12 servings)
Active Time: 30 minutes * Total Time: 1 hour, 30 minutes
Special Tools: Bundt cake pan, Ale-8-One

For the Cake:

3 sticks butter, softened

3 cups granulated sugar

5 large eggs, room temperature

3 cups all-purpose flour

1 tablespoon fresh ginger, grated

1 teaspoon ground ginger

¾ cup Ale-8-One

For the Glaze:

⅔ cup confectioners' sugar

1 tablespoon Ale-8-One

For the Cake:

Grease a 12-cup Bundt pan with butter and dust with flour. Set aside. Cream butter and sugar together using an electric handheld mixer on medium speed until light and fluffy, about 20 minutes. Add eggs one at a time, beating until completely incorporated after each egg. Sift flour into wet mixture and beat on high until batter is smooth. Fold in grated ginger, powered ginger and Ale-8. Bake at 325°F until a toothpick inserted in the cake comes out clean, about 1 hour.

For the Glaze:

Sift confectioners' sugar into medium bowl and combine with Ale-8 until glaze is shiny and smooth. Pour glaze over slightly warm cake and allow to cool. The cake is best served warm and can keep for up to 3 days covered in an airtight container.

SWEET SOUND OFF:
WADE TANDY
ALE-8 SPOKESBOY

During the 1990s and early 2000s, Ale-8 ran an ad campaign featuring a young redheaded boy asking a Pepsi salesman for a dime for his ten pennies so that he could—the Pepsi man assumed—purchase a soda from the Pepsi vending machine. When the little boy gets the dime, he uses it to purchase an Ale-8 instead, much to the chagrin of the Pepsi salesman. The ad achieved extraordinary success, and the "Got a dime, Mister?" catchphrase has become synonymous with the drink. That local child star, Wade Tandy, reflected on what it was like to be the face of Kentucky's native soda.

Tell me about your initial relationship with Ale-8.
Much like anyone who grew up where we grew up, I loved Ale-8 when I was a kid. I lived five minutes from the Clark County line, so it was a ten-minute drive to the Ale-8 factory for me. I grew up surrounded by it, so I was able to enjoy it from a very early age.

The camp I went to out in the hills of Estill County had a rule that no kids could bring soda or candy or anything like that when they went to camp for the week. However, there was an unwritten exception for anyone bringing Ale-8. You could bring all the Ale-8 you wanted, and no one would care—as long as you were kind enough to share with others—but everything else was off-limits. That's really where I first came up around it and began to really fall in love with it. We had just rows and rows and rows of the tall, green glass returnable bottles just sitting everywhere. At the end of camp, they would take them back to the factory and deposit them, and the camp would end up actually making a bunch of money off of the Ale-8 bottle profits. I'm pretty sure it's what helped keep the camp going in the summer—the deposit bottles that people brought back.

How many Ale-8s do you think you've consumed over the course of your life?
Oh god, I don't want to think about it. It's definitely in the hundreds, if not more. Seven hundred maybe, or possibly over a thousand.

When were you first approached to be in the Ale-8 commercial?
The Richmond Children's Theater was a big part of my life growing up, and I was playing one of the more prominent roles during my fourth-grade year. My dad was a partner in a company that did audio and video commercials, with his partner mainly focusing on the television side of things. My dad

had borrowed some of his partner's video equipment to film the play—as parents are wont to do—but he was really taking it to the next level with a three-camera setup and close-up shots on certain people. After the play, my dad had his partner cut together a more professional version of the play, and when he saw me acting in them, he thought I'd be really good in commercials. At the time, I'd done some radio stuff but nothing on television. He asked me to be in the Ale-8 commercial, and of course, I said yes.

Describe the day shooting the ad to the best of your memory.
We did the shoot at a little convenience store in Athens—right outside of Lexington. I was super excited to be able to take an entire morning off of school to do the shoot. It was me, the crew and the Pepsi man (who, of course, wasn't actually a Pepsi man), and while it was super fun to act and read the lines, I was really interested in the technical side of things: all the gear and cameras set up for behind-the-scenes work.

If you could describe the taste of Ale-8 in three words, what would they be?
Ale-8 tastes just like home—well, home and ginger.

What was it like to be a local celebrity?
It was super weird. Right after it happened for the first couple of years, I just thought I was the best thing that Kentucky had ever seen. I couldn't get enough of the attention.

There were actually four Ale-8 commercials that were a part of that Ale-8 campaign, and mine was only one of them. Each was a different story or situation—very charming. The campaign for all four ads was originally slated to run from anywhere between eighteen months and two years. So, I was assuming that my ad would just be on TV for two years because that's what happened with the other ads. Not so. My ad ended up airing for eight, almost nine whole years because it was really well received. I'd have people in my junior or senior year of high school say, "Hey, I saw you on TV last night!" and tease me about it. So, I definitely went through a few different cycles of how to feel about it.

Back at the camp, I got to be pretty well known for it, too. My friends would introduce me as, "This is Wade, and he's one of the guys from the Ale-8 commercial!" It was definitely a mixed bag, but good for the most part.

Have you ever thought about doing an adult version?
I would absolutely do it, but I'd be smarter this time. I'd ask them to pay me in a lifetime supply of Ale-8.

Part 5

PULLED CREAM CANDY

*H*ere's a candy riddle for you: it looks like a piece of chalk but melts in your mouth like butter. Think on it. I'll wait. Give up? It's pulled cream candy, one of the greatest confection treasures from the commonwealth. The magic of pulled cream candy all can be traced back to the unique, time-honored preparation method, which gives the fluffy-looking but hard-textured pillows of delight their signature melt-away taste.

TOOL SPOTLIGHT: MARBLE SLAB

Unless you are already a skilled candy maker (and if so, congratulations!), there's probably not a marble slab cooling its jets in your kitchen. In order to flex your cream candy muscles, though, the smooth, cool surface of the slab is a necessary tool. While marble slabs can be pretty pricey at cooking supply stores (read: upward of $100), there's a cheaper and sneakier option. Venture out to your local hardware store and purchase a marble floor tile, which is quite inexpensive and can do the job perfectly.

TIPS AND TRICKS

Chalk It Up: The texture of the creamed candy will be slightly chalky when it's ready to be cut and will hold its ridges properly.

Get Greasy: While pulling the creamed candy with buttered hands is preferable, it also raises the probability of hands getting slightly toasty (meaning burned) in the process. If you want to lower your risk, use gloves, and make sure you still butter them.

Cool Out: Ensure that your marble slab is properly cool by placing it in the refrigerator for 15–20 minutes prior to beginning the cooking process.

SIDEKICK COCKTAIL
BRANDY MILK PUNCH

Yield: 1 cocktail

1½ ounces brandy
1 ounce simple syrup
½ teaspoon vanilla extract
2 ounces half-and-half
ice
grated nutmeg, to garnish

Pour brandy, simple syrup, vanilla extract and half-and-half into a pint glass. Add ice to a shaker and shake the concoction until well mixed and frothy. Add cubed ice to a rocks glass and, using a strainer, pour the mixture into it. Top with a bit of grated nutmeg.

PULLED CREAM CANDY

Yield: 30–40 pieces
Active Time: 20 minutes * Total Time: 6 hours, 20 minutes
Special Tools: marble slab

3 cups granulated sugar
½ cup water
1 cup heavy cream
½ teaspoon baking soda

Brush a heavy-bottom saucepan with butter, attach candy thermometer, add all ingredients and bring to a boil. Cook the mixture covered, about 2 minutes, until the sugar crystals have dissolved from the sides of the pan. Remove lid and cook until candy reaches the hard ball stage, about 265°F. Pour the mixture on a buttered marble slab and let it cool enough to handle easily, about 90 seconds. Grease hands or gloves with butter and pull the candy, about 10 minutes, until it begins to set. Cut into "pillows," about 1–1½ inches long, with well-buttered scissors. Let stand for 6 hours or until completely hardened. Wrap the candy pieces in parchment paper and store in a closed tin.

SWEET SOUND OFF:
TOBY MOORE
RUTH HUNT CANDIES

Ruth Hunt Candies is synonymous with the commonwealth, having been officially designated the official candy of both Churchill Downs and the Kentucky Derby. The proud creators of more than seventy candies in Mount Sterling for almost one hundred years, Ruth Hunt's commitment to tradition and old-fashioned processes makes it a stand-alone entity on the national candy-making landscape.

How did you get involved with Ruth Hunt Candies?
My name is Toby Moore, and I've been with Ruth Hunt Candies for about twenty-five years now. I started back when the Hunt family sold the business to the Keisle family in 1988. Then Larry Keisle purchased it from my family, and I came on board at that time, and we started learning the business. At that time, I was attending my first semester in college, so not only did I not have candy experience, I didn't have any other job experiences either. Larry, on the other hand, had a career with the city government in Lexington and wanted to get his hands involved in a small business, so he purchased it. We've been here since, just trying to stay true to the time-tested recipes since there's really no need to tinker with something that isn't broken. We really just have been focusing on marketing and just spreading the word.

How did Ruth Hunt get its start?
The company started in 1921 by Ruth Hunt. At first, she just made Christmas candies, and from there, it really took off and became very popular and grew by word of mouth. In the early 1930s, she had enough business that she was able to move it out of her home and have a factory built on West Main Street in Mount Sterling. So, during what most folks remember as the Great Depression era, here she was building a factory and actually growing her business—she had to be doing something right! She was really a remarkable business lady for her time.

How did the Blue Monday candy bar get its name?
She mainly made old-fashioned candy, with one of her primary products being the old-fashioned Kentucky pulled cream candy. She made that on its own for many years, and then a few years into it, she had an idea to do a candy bar with a cream candy base. She wasn't sure what to call it until she

was talking to a traveling minister one day, and he told her how he loved to stop by the store on Mondays to get a treat to cure his "blue Monday," so she named her new candy bar the Blue Monday.

What candies do you specialize in outside of pulled cream candy?
We do a ton of traditional Kentucky candies, including the cream centers we cook in our copper kettles and the orange creams, maple creams, as well as melt-away products. We still do handmade suckers and caramels. The biggest category for business now, of course, is her bourbon ball, and we make exclusive all the bourbon balls for Woodford Reserve. We not only sell them at the distillery but all over the state and country. We started with Woodford Reserve when they first remodeled the distillery, when we were not quite sure what we were getting into. They really liked our bourbon balls, though, and at the time, they couldn't give bourbon samples away on their tours so instead they would give everyone one of our bourbon balls made with their bourbon. Everyone really loved those, and we're selling more and more Woodford products each year—we have a mint julep ball now, as well as bourbon caramel sea salt and a butter bourbon crunch.

How do you make pulled cream candy?
When people come in, most of the time they're curious and say, "What's cream candy?" and of course, the easiest thing to do is offer them a piece because it's so unique. When they read about it, though, a lot of people have a hard time understanding what you're talking about. There are several old-fashioned cookbooks with recipes for cream candy, and while it's not a difficult recipe for people to make, it is a little tricky.

Most importantly, the recipe calls for a cool marble slab. The second most important piece of equipment is a copper kettle, which is what I think allows our cream candy to cook up just right. The cream candy just has so much cream and butter in it, so the copper works really well. We have a water-cooled steel table that allows us to do multiple batches at the same time. If you used just a marble table, batch after batch, the table would begin to heat up, and you couldn't pour the mixture on it. The table with water that circulates allows us to keep a cool surface doing it in bulk.

Any tips for the actual pulling part of making cream candy?
If you pull it at home, it's a good bit of work. Years ago, we had these large hooks that were on the posts in this factory, and the ladies would just drape it over these hooks and pull it by hand. In the 1950s, we got something equal

to a taffy puller that at the time really revolutionized cream candy because they were able to go from doing it by hand to doing it by machine and were able to increase the size of the batch and do more.

After it's pulled, you have to stretch it out on the marble tables to cool, still. You have to cool it because you don't want to pull it too quickly, and you learn by doing batch after batch how to set up when you've got a short period of time to get to the pieces before it gets too hard to run through the cutter. Before that, there's the part of the process we refer to as "creaming off," where we remove the creamy top layer of the candy. A lot of local people when they know we're making a batch will come in and ask for the pulled candy "still chewy." There's about a half an hour period between when the candy is pulled and when we cream it off when it's like a totally different candy—very chewy, like a taffy. The locals really love it because it's slightly warm, and you can still taste the cream, vanilla and butter in it. Once it creams off, it stops being chewy and starts to be the really melt-in-your-mouth, creamy, smooth textures that cream candy is known for. A lot of people compare it to an opera mint or something similar to that.

What's your favorite kind of candy that you make?

I have several, and it changes from day to day, but I really like the dark chocolate caramel, the turtles, the mallows. The mallows are nice because we cook up a bunch of marshmallows, and then the ladies gather around the big copper kettles and dip them in the caramel. I like the nut clusters. I like it all, but my favorite changes every once in a while so that I don't overdo it. We do sorghum suckers, Ale-8 suckers, many different things using the same process they used back in the 1930s. For example, when you do a handmade sucker, you have a bunch of people stand around a marble table, and once the batch is cooked and put on the table, before it's cooled and set up, you take these large scissors and cut them in pieces, stick the sucker stick in it and pat it down. That process hasn't changed since they started doing it.

What kind of sweets did you eat growing up?

I've been growing up in the area and exposed to Ruth Hunt Candies my entire life. My personal tastes don't really run to the very sweet, though. I'd say I'm more a fan of an apple pie. The cream candy is really sweet, and the people who like it have that really sweet palate. The Blue Monday is unique because it has the dark, bitter, semisweet chocolate that's offset by the super-sweet center. A lot of people will tell you that they're not dark chocolate fans, but you have that contrast of a sugary center and dark chocolate outside, and they really like that because it balances it out.

Does Runt Hunt have any famous fans?
The White House called before I started working here for Blue Mondays; it was well before my time, but I'm pretty sure it was the Johnson administration that called up and ordered a big bunch. We've sent it to the Bushes—both father and son—as well as Oprah, and I'm sure there's some others. Governor Beshear is a fan as well; he enjoys our bourbon balls quite a bit from what I hear.

While taffy might be every dentist's worst nightmare (rotten teeth and dislodged crowns, oh my!), making it has an important place in Kentucky history as an autumn and springtime activity for children and teenagers. After sorghum was harvested, taffy was often made from the syrup at community events known as taffy pulling parties. The adult women would do all the difficult work—mixing, pouring and creating—but the children were able to get involved when it got really fun: pulling the taffy. Contests were frequently held to see who could pull the taffy the longest and get it to the lightest shade, in addition to the whole host of other ways to cause mischief with a hot, sticky treat (throwing it, making it into a lasso, putting it in a girl's hair and so on).

SPOTLIGHT: SORGHUM SYRUP, MOLASSES AND BEYOND

When sorghum began experiencing something of an ingredient renaissance a few years ago, many people erroneously believed that their normal, everyday molasses was the same thing as all-too-precious sorghum syrup. Not so. While both have similar traits (brown, gooey, good on biscuits), their histories and means of production are entirely separate from each other.

Sorghum: The sorghum plant is a type of grass that was introduced into the United States from Africa in the early 1600s. The plant is incredibly tolerant of heat and poor soil, which has made it a staple crop for rural communities not only in Kentucky but also across the world. Sorghum syrup is a natural sweetener made by processing the juice that is extracted from the sorghum plant. Special milling equipment extracts the juice from the crushed stalks, and it is then poured into evaporating pans with heating units that steam off the excess water, leaving only syrup. Sorghum has a sweeter taste than molasses with a thinner consistency, making it an ideal accompaniment for both baking and pouring over corn bread.

Molasses: Molasses is the byproduct created when sugars are being extracted from sugar cane and sugar beets. It can vary a great deal in color and sweetness, depending on how much sugar has been extracted. Molasses was introduced to the United States a little later during the 1800s, making its way from the Caribbean to the United States primarily for use in the sweetening of rum. The sugar cane plant is stripped of its leaves, and the juice is extracted from the cane by crushing or mashing. The juice is boiled to concentrate it, which produces crystallization of the sugar. The result of the first boiling is called "light molasses" and is the sweetest-tasting, most

> **Other Gooey, Sweet Treats**
> honey, cane syrup, maple syrup

palatable molasses for syrups and baking. The second boiling of the molasses creates "dark molasses," which has a deeper, smokier flavor and fewer sugar crystals. "Blackstrap molasses" is the result of a third boiling of the syrup. This variety of molasses contains the least sugar and has the highest concentration of vitamins and minerals. Due to the fact that Blackstrap is highly concentrated, it has a deep, spicy flavor.

TIPS AND TRICKS

Storing Sorghum: Sorghum and molasses may be stored on the shelf for up to two years, unopened. It can be stored up to a year in the refrigerator once opened unless mold appears. If the sugars in the syrup begin to crystallize, place the sorghum jar in a pot of boiling water, stirring frequently until the hardened areas are once again liquefied.

Greasy Hands: Unlike with other candies, taffy should be pulled with bare hands, not gloves. Grease hands with unsalted butter to ensure that the hot candy doesn't stick to the skin.

SIDEKICK COCKTAIL
SORGHUM COLONEL

Yield: 1 cocktail

1½ ounces bourbon
¾ ounce Amaretto
½ ounce sorghum simple syrup (¼ ounce sorghum plus ¼ ounce warm water)
cherry, for garnish

Shake all ingredients with ice. Strain into a cocktail glass. Garnish with a cherry.

SIDEKICK RECIPE
DANNY RAY'S SORGHUM OVEN CORN

Inspired by Danny Ray Townsend and his favorite way to eat sorghum, here's a variation on an addictive, Cracker Jack®—style treat.

Yield: 5 quarts popcorn, popped
Active Time: 10 minutes * Total Time: 1 hour
Special Tools: air popper

1 cup unpopped popcorn
1 cup sorghum
1 cup unsalted butter
1 cup dark brown sugar
1½ teaspoons salt
½ teaspoon baking soda
½ cup unsalted peanuts

Preheat oven to 250°F. Pop the popcorn in an air popper and then remove any unpopped kernels. Spread the popped corn onto baking sheets. Place in the oven to warm. Attach a candy thermometer to a heavy-bottom saucepan. Combine sorghum, butter, sugar and salt in the pan, stirring consistently until the mixture reaches "hard ball" stage, 266°F. Remove mixture from the heat and stir in baking soda, causing the mixture to foam. Remove corn from oven and pour hot mixture over it evenly, stirring for even distribution. Sprinkle with nuts and stir. Return to oven for 45 minutes, stirring the mixture and rotating the pan in the oven every 15 minutes. Cool and serve immediately or store in an airtight container for up to a week.

SORGHUM TAFFY

Yield: about 1 pound
Active Time: 1 hour * Total Time: 1 hour
Special Tools: candy thermometer, 9x13-inch baking sheet

2 cups sorghum
¼ cup unsalted butter
1 teaspoon vanilla extract
1 teaspoon white vinegar
½ teaspoon baking soda

Grease baking sheet with butter. Attach candy thermometer to the side of a heavy-bottom saucepan. Combine sorghum and butter in saucepan over low heat, stirring constantly to prevent mixture from sticking, until completely combined. Bring the mixture to a boil until it reaches "hard ball" stage, 266°F (mixture will be brittle and crackly when dropped into a bowl of cold water). Remove from heat and stir in vanilla and vinegar until evenly distributed. Add baking soda and mix until completely combined. Pour mixture onto greased baking sheet. Lightly butter hands and pull as soon as candy can be handled, about 60 seconds after pouring. Pull until it becomes light brown in color. Cut into 1-inch pieces using well-buttered scissors. Leave as long taffy pieces or shape into small circles. Wrap with parchment paper and store in a cool, dry place.

Sweet Sound Off:
Danny Ray Townsend
Townsend Sorghum Mill

As a native Kentucky crop, sorghum is processed at sorghum mills, where workers subscribe to largely the same extraction process for this naturally sweet syrup as their great-grandparents did hundreds of years ago. In Jeffersonville, Kentucky, Danny Ray Townsend upholds his family tradition by creating an award-winning syrup known throughout the country for its purity and delicious taste.

Talk a little bit about your family's history with sorghum.
Well, I'm the fifth-generation sorghum maker from my family here at Townsend Sorghum Mill. We've been producing sorghum for something over one hundred years now here in Jeffersonville, Kentucky, in Montgomery County.

What does sorghum taste like?
Sorghum has a taste all of its own—it doesn't taste like anything else. It's really sweet. There's three types of sorghum plant. One type that's grown out west that's just for grain that grows about five feet tall. Forage sorghum grows tall, but it's not very sweet. Then there's sweet sorghum, what we grow, that grows tall and is perfect for juicing. We're after that juice. On the sweetness scale, it's sweeter than apples. It takes about eight gallons of juice to make one gallon of syrup. The thickness of it is about equal to honey—it's a whole lot thicker than maple syrup.

How has the sorghum-making process changed over the years?
The process is basically the same, with the main thing that's changed over the years being the heat source. Back when my grandfather and great-grandfather were making sorghum, they cooked it outside in evaporator pans that were nine or ten feet long. They would use wood to power the furnace and usually use a mule but sometimes horses to power the mill. Now, we actually have a diesel engine that powers our mill and a steam boiler that produces the steam that we use to cook our sorghum. We've come from wood to natural gas to propane, and now we're cooking with steam. We grow about fifty acres of sorghum a year.

Why do you think sorghum has gained popularity in recent years?

Folks are really trying to get away from processed sugars—the so-called corn syrup or corn sugar—and instead they want something natural. Sorghum is totally natural. All we remove are the waste products and a little bit of the water. Sorghum contains no artificial anything—colors, preservatives, flavorings, nothing like that at all. Nowadays, people who are health-conscious are looking for something pure like that, which is why I think it's gaining so much in popularity.

What's your favorite thing to make with sorghum?

There's a million ways to cook with sorghum, but I would have to say my favorite is an oven caramel corn. It tastes just like Cracker Jacks®, only about ten times better. I also like cooking with sorghum in cookies and cakes; I like it on biscuits and in my beans and barbeque sauce. [With] sorghum, you can use it as a sugar substitute and even in some recipes that call for molasses because it's going to be a lot sweeter. Dressings, salads, meats—you name it. You can do anything with sorghum.

Do you think sorghum is better than molasses? Why?

Molasses is a byproduct of the sugaring process; it comes from sugar cane. That's what is left over after they take all the granulated sugar they can out of it…and what's left is that molasses: just a thick, black, really strong-tasting syrup. Sweet sorghum, on the other hand, doesn't have to go through that process. The only thing we do to make the syrup is put it in a pan and heat it up to remove the impurities. It contains all its natural sugars and is about ten times sweeter than molasses. In the day, though, some sorghum makers probably weren't very good, and they made a strong, dark syrup from a wrong cook, and then people started calling sorghum molasses. The sorghum plant can also grow this far north in Kentucky—the sugar cane plant can only grow in a subtropical climate.

What is sorghum's nutritional value?

Sorghum is very healthy. It's high in potassium and protein.

Bibliography

Aller, Joan E. *Cider Beans, Wild Greens, and Dandelion Jelly: Recipes from Southern Appalachia*. Lexington: University of Kentucky Press, 2005.

Benedict, Jennie C. *The Blue Ribbon Cookbook*. Lexington: University of Kentucky Press, 2008.

Brodowsky, Pamela K., and Tom Philbin. *Two Minutes to Glory: The Official History of the Kentucky Derby*. Louisville, KY: Churchill Downs Inc., 2009.

Bryan, Lettice. *The Kentucky Housewife*. Carlisle, MA: Applewood Books, 2001.

Carr, Sister Frances. *Shaker Your Plate: Of Shaker Cooks and Cooking*. Sabbathday Lake, ME: United Society of Shakers, 1985.

Farr, Sidney Saylor. *More than Moonshine: Appalachian Recipes and Recollections*. Pittsburgh, PA: University of Pittsburgh Press, 1983.

Flexner, Marion W. *Out of Kentucky Kitchens*. Lexington: University of Kentucky Press, 2010.

The Foxfire Book of Appalachian Cookery. Chapel Hill: University of North Carolina Press, 1992.

Gardner, Jennifer Evans, and Linda K. Jackson. *Meringue*. Layton, UT: Gibbs Smith, 2012.

Guetig, Peter R., and Conrad D. Selle. *Louisville Breweries: A History of the Brewing Industry in Louisville, Kentucky*. Louisville, KY: Mark Skaggs Press, 1995.

Long, Genevieve. *The Blue Grass Cookbook: A Manual for Housewives*. N.p.: self-published, 1903.

Lundy, Ronni. *Shuck Beans, Stack Cakes, and Honest Fried Chicken*. New York: Grove/Atlantic, Incorporated, 1994.

Meyer, Arthur L. *Baking Across America*. Austin: University of Texas Press, 1998.

Morris, Bonnie Marie. *Mountain Cooking: Recipes from Appalachia*. Seattle, WA: Createspace Independent Publishing, 2009.

O'Dell, Earleen Rather. *The Flavour of Home: A Southern Appalachian Family Remembers*. Johnson City, TN: Overmountain Press.

Odor, Mary Jordan. *So You're Going to Cook!* Louisville: National Youth Administration for Kentucky, 1939.

Okihiro, Gary. *Pineapple Culture: A History of the Tropical and Temperate Zones*. Berkeley: University of California Press, 2010.

O'Malley, Mimi. *It Happened in Kentucky*. Guilford, CT: Globe Pequot Press, 2006.

Rehder, John B. *Appalachian Folkways*. Baltimore, MD: Johns Hopkins University Press, 2004.

Rennick, Robert M. *Kentucky Place Names*. Lexington: University of Kentucky Press, 1998.

Reynolds, Mayme Miracle. *Cooking with Love and Memories in Kentucky*. Berea, KY: self-published, 1991.

Scaggs, Deirdre A. *The Historic Kentucky Kitchen*. Lexington: University of Kentucky Press, 2013.

Sohn, Mark. *Appalachian Home Cooking: History, Culture, and Recipes*. Lexington: University of Kentucky Press, 2005.

Willigen, Anne Van, and Jon Van Willigen. *Food and Everyday Life on Kentucky Family Farms, 1920–1950*. Lexington: University of Kentucky Press, 2009.

Wright, George C. *Life Behind a Veil: Blacks in Louisville, Kentucky, 1865–1930*. Baton Rouge: Louisiana State University Press, 1985.

List of Recipes

A

B

C

L

Lemon Rosewater Squares 126
Limoncello 144

M

May Day Pie 72
Mile High Lemon Meringue Pie 148
Mint Julep 70
Mint Julep Brownies 71
Modjeskas 116

O

Orange Blossom Bread 156
Orange Blossom Sangria 155
Orange Blossom Water 157

P

Pawpaw Bread 52
Pawpaw Ice Cream 50
Persimmon Pudding 46
Pickled Grapes 125
Pulled Cream Candy 171

S

Serviceberry Jam 47
Shaker Lemon Pie 128
Slow Cooker Apple Butter 62
Sorghum Colonel 178
Sorghum Taffy 180
Spiked Apple Cider 28
Spoonbread 80

T

W

About the Author

Sarah Baird is a writer, culinary anthropologist and Kentucky native whose passion for the intersection of culture and cuisine has guided her path, fork in hand, since birth. Her food writing has appeared in numerous publications, including *Serious Eats*, *Southern Living* and the *Local Palate*, as well as CNN's "Eatocracy" blog and beyond. She currently makes her home in New Orleans.